JUL 0 2 2009

D0500553

HIDING

in the

SPOTLIGHT

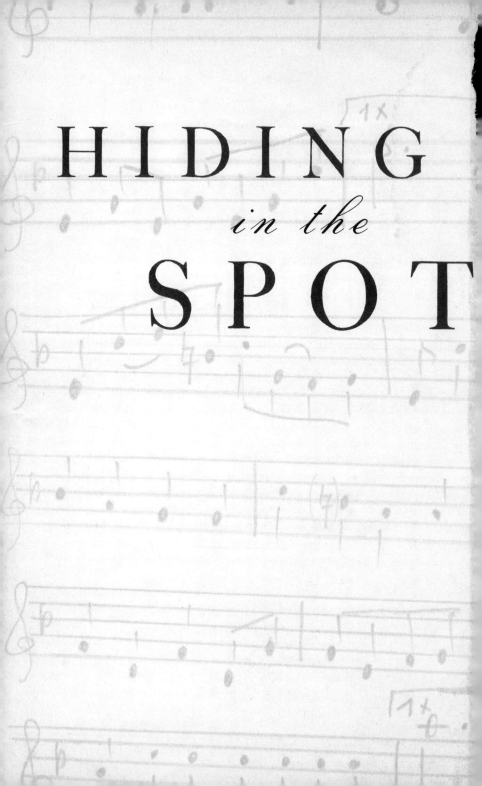

HIDING
in the
SPOT

LIGHT

A MUSICAL PRODIGY'S STORY OF SURVIVAL,

1941–1946

GREG DAWSON

PEGASUS BOOKS

NEW YORK

HIDING IN THE SPOTLIGHT
Pegasus Books LLC
80 Broad St., 5th floor
New York, NY 10004

First Pegasus Books edition

Library of Congress Cataloging-in-Publication Data is available.

Designed by Lorie Pagnozzi

ISBN: 978-1-60598-045-4

Printed in the United States of America
Distributed by W. W. Norton & Company, Inc.
www.pegasusbooks.us

10 9 8 7 6 5 4 3 2

My first lesson: you won't even
let me touch the keyboard.
You have me drum my fingers against a table
to work the stone from my wrists.

We all start with stone. For you
it was the laughter of Germans as the rabbi danced.
When the rope stopped red bull-whips cracked
and the rabbi danced again—briefly resurrected
in the sleet-backed wind of your childhood.
Or say that the stone is the wind
and the wind is the cries of children
loaded in open trucks.

Even today you hate wind.
You are so still, sit such a long time
preparing to play.
Your gold watch waits silent as a heron
over the white keys.
There are days we don't give names to,
memories more vivid than the pictures
they took away when the snow was new.
You were one of 13,000
marched out of Kharkov into the storm.
You wear the watch now to remind you of the one
your father gave a guard: barter for your life.
Almost imperceptibly it rises alone over winter fields
and the music starts:

a tough, terse piece
that counts our losses.
We lose everything.

Your fingers strike out
over unmarked graves
playing for the demanding
ears of your father
music that is first of all
survival.

"SCHOOL OF MUSIC"
—THEODORE DEPPE

Author's Note

Russian last names carry different endings depending on gender. Thus, my mother's father is Dmitri Arshansky, while she is Zhanna Arshanskaya. The family collectively takes the male ending—Arshansky. All the characters in the book are real—there are no composites—but, as my mother was unable to accurately remember a few names, in those isolated cases I have invented names.

FOR MY GRANDPARENTS, GREAT-GRANDPARENTS,
AND ALL THOSE WHO PERISHED AT DROBITSKY YAR.

HIDING
in the
SPOTLIGHT

Introduction

When I was in grade school my mother was named winner of the Allied Arts piano competition in Chicago. To ensure an outcome based solely on music, without regard to the pianists' age or gender or onstage theatrics, the contestants performed behind a screen. The judges were astonished to learn that the pianist with the powerful sound they unanimously chose as the winner was a woman "about the size of a grace note," as one critic put it.

Concealment and preternatural power. These are recurring themes in descriptions of my mother's playing, as I discovered while poring over performance reviews in my research for this book with the oxymoronic title—*Hiding in the Spotlight.*

"In this day and age when it seems too many pianists' emotions are evident mostly in facial and bodily contortions," wrote the critic for a Kansas newspaper, "Mrs. Dawson's physical reserve was a refreshing change. The drama and emotion were entirely in the music, where they rightfully belong."

Milwaukee Sentinel critic Lawrence Johnson noted "her great strength," and then wrote this about her reading of Schumann's *Kreisleriana*: "Across this endlessly varied soundscape, with its streaming lyricism and thunderous passion and myriad rhythmic tangles, the pianist measured out color and texture and pulse with unshakeable decision, clarity, and purpose."

Johnson could have easily been describing the landscape of my mother's remarkable journey. *Unshakeable decision, clarity, purpose, great strength*—these are the qualities that made it possible, with the help of prodigious talent and a family of Righteous Gentiles, for my mother to survive the Holocaust.

Years ago I managed to get a New York literary agent on the phone to deliver a quick pitch for the book. The agent was not interested; in fact, she seemed annoyed I had wasted her time. In a brusque been-there-read-that tone, she told me the genre was glutted and my only hope was to put myself in the story—make it an Oprah Book Club-friendly psychodrama about the trauma of growing up as the child of a Holocaust survivor.

In that case, I thought, my mother's story would never be told. The fact that my mother is a Holocaust survivor did not traumatize or alienate me throughout my youth, and for a very good reason—she never mentioned it. Neither did my father, a Virginian she married two years after arriving with her sister Frina in New York on the first shipload of Holocaust survivors to reach America after the war in May 1946.

That's not to say there weren't hints. At some point I did become aware that my mother was different from the other moms in our Indiana neighborhood. She spoke Russian to me as well as English and practiced the piano for hours every day. At night I lay in bed and was lulled to sleep by Chopin, Brahms, or Dvorak wafting up from the living room. My mother was dark-complected—an echo of the Mongol hordes which invaded and occupied parts of Russia in the thirteenth century—and my own mocha complexion set me apart from my fair-skinned playmates. When I was about six years old, a new kid on the block observed that I looked "dirty." A friend who knew my exotic background piped up in my defense. "He's not dirty—he's Russian."

Though I grew up acutely aware of my Russian-ness and with the vague knowledge that my mother had been through a war, I had no inkling I was Jewish, or even what a Jew was. Like the Holocaust, it was never mentioned by my mother or my father, a lapsed Catholic. All I knew about religion is that we did not go to church, which put me in another minority group amongst my childhood peers. When asked to stay for dinner at a friend's home and the family paused to say grace, I stared down at my lap, embarrassed at not knowing the words. But I was hardly traumatized.

In fact, "trauma" as we know it today—the farrago of horrific abuses, dysfunctions, and dangers that parade across our TV screens nightly—was absent from my childhood. There were no Amber Alerts or faces on milk cartons. The only "terror" was on the midnight horror show on Channel 8. Life in Bloomington, Indiana, in the 1950s and early '60s for me and my friends was not so different from the "Leave It to Beaver" fantasy, though our homes were not as nice and our parents not as well-pressed as Ward and June Cleaver.

We played kick-the-can at dusk in the parking lot of the neighborhood grocery. We cut through back yards and gravel alleys to each other's homes where we watched the *Roy Rogers Show* and sang Happy Trails as the credits rolled. We went trick-or-treating without adult escorts and returned with pillow cases full of candy our parents felt no need to check for razor blades or drugs. We raced push, scooters on the sidewalk, shot marbles for keeps, played Cowboys and Indians, and blasted each other with Lone Ranger cap pistols. In grade school I walked home for lunch and back again, alone, along tree-shaded sidewalks.

No mention, no trace of the Holocaust ever shadowed this Rockwellian tableau. A few years ago I asked my mother why, unlike so many survivors who felt a duty to pass this sorrowful torch to their children, she had not shared with me this most important chapter in her life. Her answer was simple: "How can you tell children about such things? I thought it would be too cruel."

I never heard the word Holocaust in our home, and I don't think it even entered my consciousness until my teens in the mid-1960s. Maybe even more remarkable than my mother's determined silence on the subject was the fact that I did not learn about it some other way. Today, forty years later, with the Holocaust firmly rooted in our culture as a publishing phenomenon and as grist for Hollywood directors and middle-school teachers alike, it is hard to imagine that even the most inattentive twelve-year-old does not know the name of the iconic cataclysm of our time.

Therefore, my childhood could be aptly described by the old cliché: blissful ignorance. But the ignorance was neither willful nor a matter of circumstance, as if we lived in some remote, benighted hinterland cut off from civilization. Bloomington is fifty miles south of Indianapolis, the state capital, and is the home of Indiana University. Hoagy Carmichael wrote "Stardust" there. Ernie Pyle learned journalism, Alfred Kinsey discovered sex, and Crest vanquished tooth decay. Compared with Muncie, Indiana, the subject of the famous Middletown, USA study, Bloomington was an oasis of culture, technology, and progressive, even controversial, thinking in the '50s and early '60s.

Both my parents taught at the renowned Indiana University School of Music, only a short walk through the wooded campus from the Kinsey Institute where beautiful music of a different sort was studied. I was a Crest Kid, one of 1,200 Bloomington schoolchildren used by IU researchers as guinea pigs to prove the effectiveness of fluoride in toothpaste ("Look, Mom! No cavities!"). For a period in the 1950s, every color TV set manufactured in the U.S. was assembled at the RCA plant in Bloomington. Our first TV was a 21-inch black-and-white set my father won in a drawing at the grand opening of a shoe store on the town square. I was a member of the first TV generation and took my membership seriously, starting my viewing day with test patterns at dawn. I read the newspaper (mostly to follow IU basketball) and watched the news on TV. We discussed current events at the dinner table, and my parents' conversation was peppered with the names of famous musicians, many of them colleagues at the School of Music, and most of them Jewish. Bernstein, Perlman, Gingold, Oistrah, Rostropovich—all were household names, some were after-concert cocktail guests. My mother always said, only half jokingly, that my father, who left Virginia at fourteen to attend Juilliard and fell in love with New York and all things Jewish, was the best Jew she knew. But somehow this immersion in Jewish culture—music, food, humor—never led to any talk of what happened to Jews during the war, or my mother's personal history.

Nor do I recall being taught anything about the Holocaust in grade school or junior high. As I remember it, history was presented to us as a neat succession of events, a heroic continuum beginning with the Magna Carta, followed by the Pilgrims, 1776, Gettysburg, and the wars (all just and victorious) to defend democracy and contain Communism. The world map which hung down from the chalkboard invariably had the U.S. in the center, big and pink, and the rest of the world scattered to the sides, with wide swatches of oceanic blue seeming to buffer America from the dangers that beset all other societies.

This was before the Vietnam War and the Cuban missile crisis and the assassination of John Kennedy. Before Selma and Memphis and Munich. Maverick, Mickey Mantle, *MAD*— the magazine, not the nuclear doctrine—this was my world as a child, and the murder of six million people, my grandparents included, was not part of it. My mother wanted it that way, and was so determined to preserve the façade of normalcy that I was fifty years old before I learned the true date of her birthday. It was not December 25, the day our family had always celebrated it, but, in fact, April 1—a birthday she proudly shares with her own personal god, Rachmaninoff.

Now that my mother has shared her story with me, I understand why she maintained the fiction all those years and allowed us to celebrate her birthday on the most Christian of holidays. Something so simple as a birthday was a loose thread. If it were pulled, the elaborate tapestry of her benign deception would unravel, revealing the true picture of a remarkable survivor story, but also unspeakable horrors.

"How can you tell children about such things? It would be too cruel."

So she didn't. And every year on Christmas Day we sang Happy Birthday and blew out candles on a cake.

Over the past decade, events conspired to coax my mother into revealing more and more of her story. The most crucial event was her discovery of two cousins in Israel who had never given up hope of finding her and her sister, Frina, even though it was widely assumed that both sisters died with their parents and grandparents at Drobitsky Yar, one of the Nazi killing fields in eastern Ukraine. Indeed, their names are still recited in the haunting Children's Hall at Yad Vashem, Israel's Holocaust Memorial, as my wife Candy and I discovered when we visited my mother's lone surviving cousin, Tamara, and two childhood friends, Ada and Irina, who play a significant role in my mother's story.

The day the Nazis routed the Jews of Kharkov from their homes, my mother slipped the sheet music for her favorite Chopin, *Fantasy Impromptu*, under her shirt and carried it with her through the war and to America. She still has it today, five weathered sheets, a treasured token of a lost childhood, and a piece whose name—*Fantasy Impromptu*—eerily presaged her wartime odyssey.

Like the faded sheet music, my childhood memory bears an indelible imprint, and I have come to understand that during all those years when my mother chose not to speak of her experience, she was not truly silent. She was speaking to me every night as I lay in bed in the dark—speaking in a voice that was powerfully, ferociously, and defiantly alive.

"Miss Arshanskaya is almost self-effacing," wrote a critic in 1962. "She is content to speak to her listeners only through the notes she plays."

But now, finally, the thread has been pulled, and my mother has given voice to a story that must be told. She is pleased to help preserve the story for future generations, and positively delighted, sixty-seven years after relinquishing it, to have her real birthday back and to be blowing out candles on April 1. Somewhere, Sergei Rachmaninoff is offering one of his rare, wan smiles.

Prelude

My name is Anna Morozova. I am from Kharkov. My sister Marina and I are orphans. Our father was an officer in the Red Army and was killed in action. Our mother died in the bombing of Kharkov.

She had repeated it so many times, it had become a night-marish echo in her head that would not stop.

My name is Anna Morozova. . .

This was all that was left of her life now, these five sentences. The war and the Nazis had taken everything else. Everything except the sheet music she tucked inside her shirt in the final moments before fleeing her home at gunpoint. For six months she and her sister had been running, hiding, and surviving. To everyone they met—countrymen who gave them shelter in their homes, farmers who offered rides in the backs of their wagons, Nazi soldiers who stopped them on the road, the director of an orphanage—she told the same story.

My name is Anna Morozova. I am from Kharkov. My sister Marina and I are orphans. Our father was an officer in the Red Army and was killed in action. Our mother died in the bombing of Kharkov.

She had repeated it so often, with such urgency and conviction, there were times she almost believed it was true.

My name is Anna Morozova. . . .

It was true that she and her sister were orphans from Kharkov. The rest was a lie. Their names were not Anna and Marina Morozova. Their father was not an officer in the Red Army. Their mother did not die in the bombing of Kharkov. Their real names were Zhanna and Frina Arshanskaya. Their father was a candy maker. They were Jews.

The last time Zhanna saw her parents was on a cruelly cold January morning, just after New Year's 1942. She was fourteen. The Jews of Kharkov were being marched somewhere in neat columns. The Nazis said they were going to a labor camp, but Zhanna's father didn't believe it. He bribed a guard, and the sisters escaped. They were sheltered by a family of courageous gentiles who helped them to reinvent their life as non-Jews.

My name is Anna Morozova. . . .

Only by living a lie had the sisters survived. Zhanna and Frina Arshanskaya ceased to exist. They addressed each other only as Anna and Marina. One slip, a single unguarded moment, could unmask the charade and prove fatal. Luckily, they were already disciplined performers—piano prodigies whose home was on the stage. Unluckily, their gift kept thrusting them into the spotlight where they could be spotted and betrayed at any moment.

They found their way to Kremenchug, a small Ukrainian town about 150 miles southeast of Kiev, and for a while lived in grateful anonymity in an orphanage. Then one day the startled director heard the girls playing Chopin on an old piano, and word of the precocious orphans quickly spread. They were compelled to audition for the director of the town's music school, who promptly added them to a musical troupe that performed in the town theater. Soon, Zhanna was asked to perform solo.

But she would not be playing for townspeople—the musical troupe was not for them. It was exclusively for the amusement of Nazi troops occupying the town. The soldiers were bored and needed some diversion besides drinking and carousing. Zhanna would be performing for the very people responsible for destroying her family and everything she knew. But she had no choice—to refuse would only raise suspicions.

For her first solo concert Zhanna wore a knee-length white silk dress. Her hair was in pigtails. In the darkened concert hall sat six hundred uniformed soldiers.

"Gentlemen," the theater director announced, "for your pleasure this evening, performing Chopin's Scherzo in B-flat Minor—Miss Anna Morozova!"

Zhanna entered to polite applause and curious stares. She was the troupe's first solo performer. All musical acts up to that point had been ensembles. Zhanna paused at center stage, faced the soldiers and bowed, as she was trained to do. An artist does not forget her training, no matter the circumstances. She settled herself at the grand piano and looked down, hands in her lap, communing with the keyboard, summoning all her strength for the biggest performance of her fifteen years. Would it be her last? Was she betraying the memory of her family by performing for such an audience?

In the silent interstice she heard her father's voice, the last words he said to her before she escaped the death march. "I don't care what you do—just live!"

If that meant playing for the enemy, she thought, so be it.

Ready now, she looked up, took a final sideways glance at the soldiers, and raised her hands to the keyboard. . . .

Chapter One

The room was slowly filling with the first gray light of morning when Zhanna awoke. As she did almost every night, Zhanna had fallen asleep in the living room to a lullaby of Rossini and Strauss, Bizet and Tchaikovsky. Her father, Dmitri, on violin, and his good friend, Nicoli, at the piano, played deep into the night, their sheet music illuminated by candles and kerosene lamps. Zhanna and her younger sister, Frina, shared a bedroom, but on the nights Nicoli came to play, Zhanna never saw her bed.

I enjoyed the music so much, they wouldn't dare to put me to bed anywhere but the living room. The decision was made to put a bed in the living room for me. Evenings meant music with my father and Nicoli. Every night was a celebration. I would go outside and wait on the corner for Nicoli to come. I would run to him and he would throw me in the air. We would go inside and sit down and the music would begin. Often he would let me climb up and sit in his lap as he played.

Zhanna was always the first one up in the Arshansky home and this morning was no different. Moving gingerly so as not to wake her parents, she went about her daily routine. There was no time to lose. No time even to eat. The empty streets beckoned! It was a chilly November day in southern Ukraine, so Zhanna put on the white woolen suit and hat that she loved so much. Quietly closing the door and stepping outside into the sharp air, she felt a rush of excitement at the prospect of visiting the bazaar, all her favorite streets and, of course, the apothecary shop. The only thing standing between 3½-year-old Zhanna and a day of adventure was, as usual, the locked door of the front gate. She was not tall enough to open it, even on tiptoes, but had learned how to climb up and undo the heavy latch. She was not to be denied. She had places to go and things to do!

I spent a tremendous amount of time by myself because nobody could stand my company. I had to go where I had to go. I had to see what I had to see. I was born busy—eaten up by curiosity. Nothing could stop me. I was part of the environment and I was sure it couldn't be any other way. The place was made for me, it was mine. I was kind of occupying the city.

Standing on the corner, a tiny bundle of white wool with stubby legs, Zhanna considered her options for the day. There was never enough time to go all the places she wanted to go, to see all the things she wanted to see. The bazaar, the beaches, the churches, the shops, the hospital, the cemetery on a high hill overlooking the city. If her mind and senses had a mecca to which they always turned it was the apothecary where she admired the array of medicine bottles and was mesmerized by the pharmacists plying their mysterious art.

I would try to look in the windows, but they were too tall, so I would walk up the steps and get closer where I could see the people working, mixing things. I adored the little containers. I would go home and find bottles and pretend to do chemistry and make up colors. That was my play. I never played with dolls. I didn't know what to do with a doll.

Berdyansk was Zhanna's only toy, a personal amusement park where she never had to wait in line. It was a cloistered resort town on the Sea of Azov, a shallow body of sapphire water connected by the narrow Kerch Strait to the vast Black Sea to the south. It was a place of small houses on quiet, shaded streets, of merchants and fishermen and horse-drawn carriages. There were no cars and few bicycles. Zhanna never saw a plane in the sky. Summertime tourists arrived by train or boat, lured by miles of sandy beaches and the famous mud-cure therapy. The loudest sounds were the clip-clop of horses' hooves on cobblestone, the hum of the bazaar, and occasional cheers from a soccer game.

It was so quiet. I sat on the beach inspecting shells, listening to the transparent waves rolling in and out, producing their calming splash, arriving and returning to the sea. The town was the description of peace itself. I could feel it in my small bones.

In the late 1920s, Berdyansk was a place where a child could safely walk the streets alone—though sometimes at the end of the day an amused Zhanna would be carried home in the arms of a fretful policeman and handed over to her chagrined parents, who searched in vain for a cure to her raging wanderlust.

Situated along the approximate longitude of Turkey and Egypt, the region had a kaleidoscopic history, each twist of fate producing new and colorful—often exotic—cultural and political patterns, starting before Christ with the Scythians and Sarmatians and proceeding to successive reigns by the Slavs, the Golden Horde of Genghis Kahn, the Cossacks, and finally the Russians. In perhaps the most antic chapter, a group led by Ukrainian revolutionary Nestor Makhno established an anarchist society in an area of Ukraine that included Berdyansk from late 1918 to June 1919.

Founded in 1827 as the outgrowth of a fishing settlement, Berdyansk was perched on a small peninsula with a wide sand bar that reached five miles into the Azov, beckoning visitors and providing a hospitable home for marine life. Fed by the Don and Kuban rivers, the warm, shallow waters of the Azov were a fisherman's paradise, teeming with sturgeon, perch, bream, mullet, herring, sardines, and anchovies—the stuff of many meals in the Arshansky home. The town grew apace with the busy seaport which shipped tons of wheat from local Mennonite and German communities. Mirroring the eclectic parade of rulers and influences, the city was born Kutur-Ogly and later renamed Novo-Nogaisk before becoming Berdyansk in 1842.

Zhanna's favorite time was summer, when Berdyansk was in full bloom and the sea was warm and the days deliciously long.

She hit the streets at dawn, wearing only a skimpy bathing suit or panties and no shoes, and was swept along by her senses.

> *In early morning you could expect each flower to exude*
> *the most potent smell: acacia, roses, lily of the valley.*
> *Night flowers, morning flowers—the most marvelous*
> *aromas. I would go to the bazaar before the sun was*
> *completely up. People would bring magnificent things*
> *to sell. The best yogurt, with a beautiful brown crust*
> *on top, eggs and cream and butter, gorgeous, aromatic*
> *fruit—pears so big they had to be cut in a bowl to catch*
> *the delicious juice —roasted sunflower seeds, fish caught*
> *in the Sea of Azov that very day.*

Tourists bought strings of smoked and sun-dried fish and bub-liki—bagels—and wore them around their necks as they strolled through the market. Zhanna mingled easily with the visitors and always had an eye and ear open for new adventures. Once on a panties-only day she encountered a funeral procession—a horse-drawn wagon bearing a coffin, Orthodox priests in golden robes swinging lanterns, and a small band playing a funeral march. Zhanna was transfixed. The music called to her. She had to join the procession. At the church the mourners invited her—barefoot and half-dressed—to sit with them inside. It was the first time she had seen the interior of a church or synagogue.

> *They were all dressed and I was just in panties. How*
> *tolerant they were to let me be present at their most*
> *sacred of times. Every speck of the church was gilded,*

lavish. There were icons everywhere and mosaic windows. It was so gorgeous. I felt like I was already in heaven.

After that, she could never resist the funeral dirge. It was her Siren song. She had to fall in line. For a Jew whose family never went to synagogue, Zhanna spent a lot of time in church, tagging along to every funeral she could.

The music was the magnet. It was the same funeral march, the one for all the common people. It broke my heart every time. I would get the biggest tears and would walk with the family, crying for their relatives. I was absolutely obliged to go.

Like her independence, Zhanna's curiosity knew no bounds and she was not squeamish. If she wasn't in church mourning the dead, she might be at the hospital with the nearly dead.

I would see a person being taken in a horse cart to the hospital, head hanging off the cart. I couldn't tell if he was dead or alive, so my planned destination that day would be changed to follow the cart to the hospital to see if he was dead. For some reason I had to know. Had to know . . . had to go . . . had to see.

Little Zhanna lived life in the imperative mood. She was a cheeky child with a round face and plump brown cheeks, an inveterate teaser, and a tester of limits.

My grandmother was a person of limitless patience.
One day she and I were the only ones at home. We
were sitting at the long kitchen table where my father
made candy and where we ate meals and played cards.
Grandmother was knitting and talking with me. I
decided to test her patience and tolerance. I picked up a
very heavy brass mortar and pestle and started beating
them together to see how long she could stand it. But
it was I who had to give up when I lost my power.
She kept knitting as though there was peace and quiet,
almost as though she knew exactly what I was trying to
do—exasperate her.

Zhanna rejected peace and quiet the way nature abhors a vacuum. She was instinctively drawn to—challenged and goaded by—the locked gate, the high window, the blind alley . . . and the word no. When her mother, Sara, was pregnant with her, she read the Russian translation of Mark Twain's *Joan of Arc* and decided that if the baby was a girl she would be named for the book's courageous and defiant heroine. "Zhanna" was the closest Russian equivalent to Joan. On the day Zhanna was born in 1927, her mother could not know that the name she chose was eerily prophetic—that Zhanna, like her namesake who was burned at the stake for heresy, one day would be called to face an enemy that used incineration as a tool of war.

But such horrors were unimaginable on a chilly autumn morning in 1930 as Zhanna Arshanskaya stood alone on the street corner, exhilarated by her freedom—the world at her tiny feet. Who knew what discoveries and delights lay ahead that

day? She glanced down the street in the direction of the Orthodox church, then the other way toward the bazaar, the shops,
and the beaches. It was a tantalizing choice, but in the next moment she knew her destination.

I must go to the apothecary!

Zhanna turned right and headed down the street with her
short but purposeful stride, a ball of white wool bouncing across
the cobblestones. The thought of the apothecary and its many
wonders made her happy. And when she returned home tonight,
Nicoli would be there! Life could not be sweeter.

Chapter Two

At the dawn of the twentieth century, Russia was home to approximately five million Jews, the greatest concentration in the world, but they were Russians first, as Polish Jews were Poles first, and as the fealty of German Jews was to Germany. The casting aside of separate national identities for a universal Jewish solidarity tied to resurrection of an ancient homeland—that tectonic shift belonged to an unimaginable future. In the 1890's, Jewish historian Simon Dubnow, who was executed by Nazis in a Latvian ghetto in 1941, lamented the benumbed memory of Russian Jews.

"Only in our midst, among the Jews of Poland and Russia, has there been kindled no desire to uncover the secrets of our past, to know what we were, how we came to our present circumstances and how our forefathers lived during the eight hundred years beginning with the start of Jewish life in Poland. There are times when I suspect in my heart that we altogether lack historical feeling—as if we were likes gypsies whose lives are entirely in the present and who have neither a future nor a past."

This was a fair description of the Arshanskys, who were Jewish by birth and culture, not by religious belief or practice. They did not attend synagogue—or any other house of worship—and there was no mention in the home of Judaism or Zionism or Palestine. There were a few traces of Jewish heritage. Dmitri and Sara sprinkled their Russian with Yiddish, and Zhanna recalls rueful references to pogroms, though their awful import was never fully explained by her parents.

The first major spasm of pogroms occurred in southern Russia in 1881 after the assassination of Czar Alexander II, for which the Jews were wrongly blamed. In more than 200 towns, Jews were killed and injured and their homes destroyed. A second wave from 1903 to 1906 killed 2,000 Jews, a paroxysm that became a frenzy during the revolution of 1917 and the Russian Civil War that followed when tens of thousands of Jews across Russia were slaughtered. One effect of the pogroms was to drive Jews away from their vulnerable hinterland shtetls to the relative safety of cities with new industry and more ethnically and culturally diverse populations. Cities provided "secular" Jews like the Arshanskys the opportunity to assimilate so seamlessly that they became indistinguishable from ethnic Russians.

Music took the place of religion in Dmitri Arshansky's home. Paganini was his god and his bible was a book with a photo of the great violinist and composer playing his instrument. A self-taught violinist, Dmitri studied the photo for hours with the grave devotion of a Talmudic scholar, holding his fiddle under his chin and attempting to mimic the master's hand positions. Observing her father in deep concentration, Zhanna silently rooted for a miracle.

*I somehow knew that my father was not the number
one violinist on the Earth, and so if he could improve
it would be good. People said it was not human to play
the way Paganini did, and my father believed it must
be in the way he held the violin. I was hoping that
one day he would find Paganini's secret. We had the
picture on the table forever. No one was allowed to
close the book.*

Dmitri never heard Paganini—phonographs were rare amenities in Ukrainian homes—nor did he dare perform any of his
compositions. To butcher the music of his god would have been
a sacrilege. Though he was no Paganini, Dmitri played well
enough to provide music at family weddings and to be part of a
small ensemble that supplied the soundtrack for silent American
movies shown at an outdoor theater in Berdyansk. And there
were the almost nightly "concerts" with Nicoli in the Arshansky living room before an enthusiastic, though sleepy, audience
of one.

If Paganini was god, and the book with his photo was the
bible, the altar in Dmitri's church of music was the piano, which
occupied center stage in the cramped living room. It was an upright model with an unusual feature: a mirror behind the music
stand. Dmitri ordered the piano from Germany. He believed
that Germans made the finest pianos; but it was not just their
craftsmanship he admired, it was their culture and their ado-
ration of music which he shared. After all, such a culture had
produced Bach, Beethoven, and Brahms. During World War I
when Germans peacefully occupied Poltava in Ukraine, young

Dmitri made friends with Yiddish-speaking German soldiers who sought out Jews for conversation. It left him with an enduring image of Germans as polite and cultured, kindred spirits.

Sara was a woman of sartorial style—she came from a family of hat makers—and eclectic intellectual curiosity. A voracious reader, she filled the Arshansky home with fine literature—Tolstoy, Chekhov, Shakespeare, Twain—encyclopedias, and color picture books of Africa, for which Zhanna developed a special fascination. She was reading, writing and reciting poetry before she was five. But for her father, nourishment of the mind was secondary to cultivation of the soul—the majestic, saturnine Russian soul which he believed drew its strength and animating spirit from music. Dmitri was determined that his daughters would become world-renowned pianists, and that they would learn on a German piano. Only the best was good enough for his future virtuosos.

Dmitri started preparing his older daughter for the stage before her legs were long enough to reach the piano pedals. He would take Zhanna to rehearsals of an amateur orchestra and playfully seat her at the piano, as if she were the guest artist for the evening.

He would say, "You play!" And I would look at the music in front of me and say, "I don't know how to play this. I cannot read this music!" He would order me to play anyway, and so I would play any notes my hands could grab. Everyone in the orchestra thought it was such a wonderful game.

There was just one flaw in Dmitri's grand plan for Zhanna: she wanted no part of it. As much as she loved listening to music, Zhanna had no innate interest in learning to play. Why go to the trouble of learning to play, when her father and Nicoli were there to perform for her every night? She did not have time to sit and practice for hours a day. Not with a city waiting to be explored. Places to go! Things to do!

When Dmitri finally put his foot down and Zhanna started lessons at age five, the reasons were practical as well as artistic, a last-ditch attempt by her exasperated parents to get her off the streets. The first plan—putting Zhanna in kindergarten— had backfired louder than the cannon in Tchaikovsky's *1812 Overture*. She already could add, subtract, multiply, and read—a common trait among the musically gifted—and was bored being surrounded by mere children.

It was a farce. I was sticking out like a sore thumb. I was too tall, too clean, too well-fed. I hated their food. I hated watching the poor, underprivileged children with colds, with their noses dripping into their pumpkin kasha. I felt miserable for them but I felt more like a teacher than one of them. I was the most arrogant thing that ever walked in there. The teachers paid no attention to me because I did not need their help. No one knew why I was there, and everyone was delighted when I started coming late. I made my walk to school very slow and pleasurable. I adored the wonderful sea pebbles on the roads and around the trees in the center of town. I would sit down and play with the pebbles, then

visit the beaches. There was a beach for horses, a beach
for women, a beach for men, and a beach for everybody.
I had to visit them all, of course.

Piano lessons might be the only way to rein in his little truant, Dmitri decided. But who would agree to teach such a child? With great trepidation he asked a family friend, Svetlana, who was a piano teacher, to come to the Arshansky home one night and meet Zhanna. They sat together at the long kitchen table.

"Let me see your hands," Svetlana said.

Zhanna extended her hands—small, plump, and dimpled.

The teacher sighed and shook her head. "I don't know what I can do with these."

"Please don't refuse to take her!" Dmitri begged. "She is walking the streets and we don't know what to do."

Zhanna was barely listening. Her focus was on a plate of butter on the table. As her father implored the teacher, Zhanna was dipping her finger into the butter and eating it. Heavenly!

"Okay," Svetlana finally said, "I will try."

Svetlana was not starting from scratch. At least her reluctant student loved music, and her subconscious was imprinted with melody, rhythm, and tempo from countless nights of drifting off to sleep as her father and Nicoli played. She already knew the names of the notes on the treble and bass staff lines and between the lines. For an eager student it would have been a priceless head start, but it left Zhanna smug and complacent.

The teacher started introducing me to leger lines—the
short lines above and below both clefs. I was so satisfied

with my great achievement of learning the notes that
I thought it was just going too far to have to learn
the leger lines as well. I made a decision not to have
anything to do with it. I hid my home assignments in
the ashes of the stove outside where my family cooked
meals in the summer.

Zhanna avoided practicing whenever possible, and turned the five-block trip to Svetlana's home into a circuitous two-hour journey. She was much more interested in her teacher's two-year-old son and his large collection of toys than she was in mastering a C-major scale. Svetlana would rap Zhanna's arm with a pencil to recapture her flagging attention. But despite herself, Zhanna was learning to play, and soon she was performing repertory which takes most students years to master. Dmitri was delighted. Friends and family gathered at the Arshansky home to hear Zhanna play. Everyone was impressed by Zhanna's precocious artistry—except Zhanna herself.

There were not many pianists in the town. Even my
teacher wasn't playing, just teaching. It was like being
the greatest beauty in a village where there is only one
woman.

Frina, age four, did not see it that way. She wanted to play like her older sister and be in the spotlight receiving bravos and attention. Sometimes when Zhanna performed, Frina would run into the next room and hide in a huge wicker basket of dirty laundry and cry. Heartbroken, Dmitri let her start lessons, but

Frina was not ready. Unlike Zhanna at the same age, she could not yet read, write, or do arithmetic, and the lessons lasted only a short time. Zhanna was always impatient for Frina to grow up.

> *Frina was the most gorgeous child you could imagine, with long, golden curls. But to me, she was always a baby. I wanted her to speak to me sooner than she could. Once we were sitting in the sandbox—I was four and she was two. I got very mad because she did not follow what I wanted her to do. I threw sand in her face and it got in her eyes. I can't stand the thought of what I did. The guilt can last a lifetime.*

A year later, when she was five, Frina resumed lessons and soon it became clear that she had the same rare gift as her sister. Zhanna, meanwhile, was rapidly developing as an artist. One day when she was six her teacher came to Dmitri and asked his permission for Zhanna to perform live on the radio. He was ecstatic! This was the realization of Dmitri's dream, which he had playfully enacted so many times by seating little Zhanna at the piano to the delight of orchestra members. But he had never expected it to happen this soon. It was not so long ago that Zhanna had been sitting on Nicoli's lap *pretending* to play, her tiny hands flying above the keys in a pianistic pantomime.

It was decided that for her radio debut, Zhanna would play Bach's Two-Part Invention No. 1 in C Major. Even though the audience could not see her, Zhanna put on a dress and nice shoes for the big event. Dmitri walked her by the hand to the radio station at the center of town, got her settled in the studio, then hurried home to listen on the radio with the rest of the family.

The studio was a small, windowless room. In the center was a lovely rug, and on it stood a grand piano. Zhanna had never seen one before. It looked enormous, but she was too young and brash to be intimidated. Did it not have the same keys, in all the same places? She climbed up onto the piano bench and waited for a signal from the technician seated behind glass in a tiny control room.

He lifted his arm, hesitating momentarily at the apex, then dropped it in a sharp chopping motion and pointed to Zhanna.

In the Arshansky living room, a nervous Dmitri nodded approvingly at the first sound of his daughter's playing, clear but tinny, coming through the speaker of the family's old radio.

Suddenly, disaster struck. Eight bars into the piece, the studio lights went out. Berdyansk's primitive power supply was off more than it was on, and was prone to random outages. Zhanna was thrown into total darkness, yet the station remained on the air. She had to keep playing! Zhanna was not using music, but even when playing from memory she was accustomed to watching her hands.

There was no time to think. I had to keep playing even though I could not see my hands on the keyboard. My father had trained me to play in the dark to ensure mastery of the keyboard. People would come to our home to hear me play, and he would close all the shutters and order me to play in complete darkness. So I knew I could do it. I played to the end without hesitation.

"Bravo! Bravo!" rang out in the Arshansky home. To Dmitri's ear it had been a flawless performance, an extraordinary debut. He had no idea just *how* extraordinary.

As Zhanna waited outside the station for her father to come walk her home, she reflected on the experience. That was fun, she thought. And satisfying. Papa would be proud. She couldn't wait to do it again!

Chapter Three

In good times, the Arshansky home was filled with the sound of music and the aroma of Dmitri's caramels bubbling on the coal-burning stove. The two were connected in a vital way. Selling his candy made it possible for Dmitri to buy a violin for himself and to order a piano and sheet music from Germany for his daughters. On the violin he was a would-be virtuoso, but at the stove, confecting his caramels and hard candies, Dmitri was a true master, carrying on an art he had learned from his father in Mariupol, his boyhood home just north of Berdyansk on the Sea of Azov.

He made hard candy in a variety of fruit flavors, but Dmitri's specialty were the caramels made with butter and cream. A one-man operation, he cooked the ingredients in two huge copper pots, then poured the syrup into pans and set them on a table by the window to cool. When the syrup hardened, he sliced it into pieces that were wrapped in wax paper at the family's long kitchen table and taken to the bazaar to be sold by vendors. They always sold out quickly.

At the end of the 1920s, businessmen like Dmitri were reaping the benefits of economic measures instituted by Lenin after

World War I to let peasants sell some produce for profit and to allow small businesses to operate as private enterprises. Under Lenin's New Economic Policy (NEP), peasants were allowed to own farmland and Russia once again became an exporter of grain, as it had been before World War I. Thanks to his thriving business, Dmitri was able to rent a modest frame house, which made the Arshanskys middle-class by standards of the supposedly classless Soviet system. By most other standards, it was a rather spartan existence.

Six people shared the small space: Zhanna, Frina, their parents, and their paternal grandparents. The house had no electric lights, no refrigeration or indoor plumbing. The family used public baths for bathing and an outhouse in the backyard. A feeble, flickering electrical current was useful only for powering the radio sporadically. Yet life seemed rich to Zhanna.

In the backyard was a shed where the family stored barrels of preserved cherries, plums, tomatoes, pickled watermelon rind, red and green apples, cucumbers and cabbage, all from the garden. Her mother made gefilte fish, and wine from cherries and prunes. A large tree shaded a wooden table where the family gathered for meals in balmy weather, cooled by breezes from the Azov. Zhanna wished at those moments that she could stop time, and that such perfect happiness could be preserved like summer cherries and plums for a darker, colder day.

But the good times did not last. Stalin seized dictatorial control of the Communist Party in 1927 and proceeded to snatch economic disaster from the jaws of modest success and incremental progress. He sought to wipe out all vestiges of the capitalism which had blossomed under Lenin's NEP that and to transform the Soviet Union into a pure socialist state through rapid industrialization and collectivized farming. This would be achieved by forcing peasants off their land onto collectivized farms ("kolkhozes") and would also serve the purpose of crippling the "kulaks," or wealthy peasants, loosely defined as anyone who owned horses and cows and produced enough food to sell in the marketplace. Though the kulaks were only five percent of the population, Stalin perceived them as the possible vanguard of a wider peasant revolt that must be strangled in the crib before it could rise up against him.

Stalin first placed his hands around the peasants' necks in 1928 by ordering the state to pay below-market prices for grain. Peasants responded by keeping their grain off the market, an act of treason to Stalin. Thousands of farmers were arrested for "hoarding," and Party officials were dispatched to confiscate grain and other property, triggering bloodshed between soldiers and peasants.

Incredibly, Stalin ordered that all Soviet agriculture would be collectivized in one year. A goon squad of 25,000 Party members, backed by regular army and police units, descended on villages to forcibly herd peasants like so many cattle to kolkhozes. Pockets of armed resistance led to thousands of deaths, executions, and the exiling of survivors to prison camps. Entire villages were burned. Some farmers resisted by destroying their own crops and slaughtering their animals.

Stalin set impossibly high quotas for kolkhozes, and when they did not deliver, authorities confiscated seed that was to be used for the next planting as punishment, thus setting in motion a vicious cycle. Harvests shrank, but Stalin still took his lion's share—and more. In 1932, the grain harvest in Ukraine was 14.4 million tons. The state took it all. Widespread hunger among peasants on the kolkhozes led to mass starvation. There were reports of cannibalism and people eating field mice, bark, and grass. Meat sold on the street was checked by police to determine if it came from a dog—or a person. Stalin posted the Red Army at the border to prevent the escape of starving citizens, lest the rest of the country learn of the catastrophic results of his policies.

No place suffered more than Ukraine. Stalin's forced famine would kill six million people in what once was known as the "breadbasket of Europe." An Estonian minister reported what he saw on a tour of the region in July 1933.

"The people at the stations looked like hordes of beggars. At every station there were great numbers of men, women, and children begging bread from passengers. I shall never be able to forget the pitiful voices of the children. When a piece of bread was thrown, scores of people would rush for it like a pack of hungry dogs."

Zhanna saw it firsthand at street level. Her once-joyful explorations of Berdyansk were now more like tours of a terrible battlefield in war.

The farmers came into Berdyansk to find food and work and they found nothing. I saw people all bundled up in winter clothes, lying on the street dying of hunger and cold—swollen to three times their normal size, and blue. One day I found two little girls in a hut close to the hospital I used to visit. They had no bed, no

parents. They were just freezing there. I ran home and
told my mother that I had to take food to those children.
She gave me some, but I knew they had no chance to
survive.

Survival had become a struggle for the Arshanskys. Dmitri's
business began to shrivel and die under the weight of higher and
higher taxes. Soon he could no longer afford to buy ingredients
to make candy, but it didn't matter because no one had money
for caramels anyway. Sara began taking household items such as
carpets and dishes to the bazaar and bartering them for flour and
other coveted staples.

Worse than hunger for Zhanna was the fear that, any day,
her father might vanish and never return. Stalin's orchestrated
famine was accompanied by a murderous purge in the 1930's
of party unfaithfuls and faithful alike—especially citizens like
Dmitri who had the temerity never to join the Communist Party.
Dmitri was repeatedly interrogated by the secret police, and was
arrested and jailed several times. It was the same terror Zhanna
had felt years before when her father went to sea with fishermen
and was caught in a great storm, and her mother stood on the
shore for hours, not speaking, staring out to sea.

Zhanna and Dmitri had a special bond. They weren't just
father and daughter; they were buddies, even look alikes. They
are standing side by side in a family photo taken when Zhanna
was eight. Dmitri is in a suit, high-collared white shirt, and tie.
He has a roundish face, handsome features, and a swarthy complexion that hints at those distant Mongol roots. His gaze behind wire-rim glasses is steady and penetrating. The corners of

his mouth are turned up in a half-smile. Zhanna's resemblance to her father is striking.

They also shared an urge to wander, and a congenial curiosity and fascination with all those who crossed their paths. Dmitri carried Zhanna on his shoulders to see silent movies in the town square, and they explored the city together.

I was kind of like a pal to my father. He hated to leave home without me. He went everywhere and talked to everybody, and I listened and learned to do the same. There was no alcohol in our house except for homemade wine, but on our outings Father would stop at a beer stand and get a big, heavy mug of beer and give me a taste. It was a special event—a father-and-daughter event.

Such carefree outings were now just a memory. Their father-and-daughter events had been reduced to this desperate scene: Zhanna standing on the corner outside their house watching for the approach of secret police, so she could warn her father inside.

I would run into the house and think, "How am I going to hide my father?" I knew all the places in the house and I was thinking, "Where can I put my father so they won't find him?" But the house was so small. I could think of only one place—but he was too big to hide in the basket of dirty laundry like Frina.

Every time the police came, they found Dmitri. Often it was a man with a limp who came. Zhanna never forgot the man with the limp.

> *That is embedded in my memory. He said to my father, "You are Jewish—you've got to be rich! Where is the gold?" Of course, we didn't have any. He would show his golden pocket watch but they had no interest in it. They wanted money—gold. They took father away so many times.*

Dmitri always came back. But it was clear that the Arshanskys could not remain in Berdyansk. The only question was which event, what final indignity, would drive them away. One day Dmitri had no more money for taxes and the authorities announced they were coming to take the family's furniture.

> *That was the last straw that broke us. I panicked at the fear of being homeless and I secretly cried—I didn't want my parents to see. We knew we had to leave before they took everything. They could have the rest, but my father was determined to save the piano and his violin.*

The Arshanskys' new home would be Kharkov, a large city 250 miles north of Berdyansk. Sara's sister, Eve, lived there with her husband, Semyon, and their two daughters, Tamara and Celia—Zhanna's cousins. There was certain to be more work for Dmitri, and he was hopeful that Zhanna and Frina could be admitted to the prestigious Kharkov Conservatory.

But leaving Berdyansk struck Zhanna at her core. It was not just the city of her birth, it was *her* city, the field of her childhood dreams and delights. She had possessed Berdyansk and would forever be possessed by it—by the sea and the sky, the acacia and the lilac, the bazaar at dawn, the haunting funeral dirge.

Not all was lost. The tax collectors could not take her memories. Her father had saved his most treasured possessions, the piano and his violin. The Arshanskys had survived Stalin's own holocaust. Zhanna strode briskly into the future, confident that life could only get better.

Chapter Four

Zhanna was infatuated with Kharkov from the start. It was an even bigger and better wonderland than her beloved Berdyansk. A city of nearly one million, Kharkov had buses, trolleys, parks, museums, a circus—Zhanna liked to wait by the entrance in hopes of glimpsing a black man like the ones in her African picture book—and a galaxy of markets and streets to be explored. The only thing missing was the sea.

Zhanna's delight in the city made it easier to accept the comedown in her family's living conditions. They had gone from the modest but cozy rented house in Berdyansk to a one-room flat in a row of slightly dilapidated apartment buildings on Katsarskaya Street in Kharkov. There was not enough room for the grandparents, who stayed behind in Berdyansk and hoped to come later. They were able to get by on money Dmitri's father saved from the sale of his home and business in Mariupol before moving to Berdyansk.

Crowded into one square room were two small beds, a couch, a rolling dresser for hanging clothes, a table and chairs, and the piano—a space-eating luxury in the tiny room. In one wall was an indentation for a wood-burning stove. The bathroom was down the hall.

It was a narrow hallway with seven apartments. The bathroom was in the middle and was shared by all seven apartments. It was just a cubbyhole with a curtain across it, halfway to the ceiling, and it was right next to the place where people prepared food. There was a terrible-looking sink, all dark like the toilet, and a little table where we put a kerosene burner to cook in the summer when it was too hot to use the stove. In the winter we always used the stove because it heated our room. We had no refrigerator or icebox—I did not even know what they were—so my mother had to shop every day at the bazaar.

There was little money for shopping. Dmitri was distressed that the only job he could find in Kharkov was lifting heavy boxes at a candy factory, and it aggravated his ailing back so severely that he had to quit. He made a meager amount from occasional stints as a last-stand violinist in the local philharmonic, and by giving piano lessons to children. The Arshanskys ate a lot of bread and sunflower oil. Dmitri no longer could afford tobacco and papers for rolling cigarettes, his only indulgence.

Their salvation, as always, was music. Zhanna had just turned nine and Frina was seven the day Dmitri took them on a short trolley ride from their flat on quiet Katsarskaya Street to teeming downtown Kharkov and the steps of the conservatory, a huge, ornate building with pillars, gold filigree, and high windows.

Dmitri led the girls up a wide staircase, pointing out framed portraits of Russian musical icons: Tchaikovsky, Prokofiev, Scriabin, Goldenweiser, Neihaus, Egumnov, Rachmaninoff, Anton and Nikolai Rubinstein. It was rarefied air for a student audition.

The portraits only began to tell the history of the region's musical genius. No place on earth produced more virtuosos per capita in the nineteenth and twentieth centuries than did Ukraine alone. From a region not quite the size of Texas sprang a cohort of legendary violinists that included Isaac Stern, Jascha Heifetz, David Oistrakh, Mischa Elman, and Nathan Milstein—the equivalent of Texas alone producing Hemingway, Faulkner, Fitzgerald, Steinbeck, and Bellow. And then there were the pianists, among them Emil Gilels, Sviatoslav Richter, and Vladimir Horowitz—as if Texas had also claimed Twain, O'Neill, and Frost.

Thankfully, the Soviet system was kinder to culture than to agriculture, far more efficient at producing pianists than wheat. While Stalin's forced collectivization was having a ruinous effect on Ukrainian farms, the system of state-sponsored music conservatories, coupled with the tradition of Russian piano pedagogy dating back to the founding of the St. Petersburg Conservatory in 1862 by Anton Rubinstein, was amazingly prolific. Starting at age seven, children could take exams and be admitted to one of more than two thousand elementary music schools or, if they were exceptionally gifted, one of two dozen conservatories for budding prodigies. From there they graduated to a secondary music school for artists. Early training focused on technique, and those who did not master it were left behind. In addition to a rigorous schedule of academic classes, the music students had classes in choir, music literature, theory, ensemble, vocal accompaniment, and chamber music. The repertory required at each level was standardized throughout the Soviet Union and included pieces written expressly for children by Russian composers such as Dmitri Kabalevsky and Alexander Gretchaninoff. Students were tested early and often to weed out the merely adequate. Out of a hundred talented young pianists, only twenty would reach the pinnacle—Moscow State Conservatory.

By the dint of their own precocity and Dmitri's unblinking pursuit of his dream, Zhanna and Frina had leapfrogged the state system and now stood, literally, on the threshold of an unprecedented opportunity. They reached the top of the stairs and entered a high-ceilinged room. Seated behind a long table was a jury of faculty members who would decide if the sisters would be admitted to the conservatory. The jury listened without expression as first Zhanna, then Frina, played.

> We had to play Bach, the one-part invention. I also
> played a prelude from Bach's Clavier and a fugue in
> another key. Bach is God in Russia. If you don't know
> Bach, you don't know music. And of course we had to
> play scales. In Russia, scales are much more important
> than in American schools. Scales teach you everything
> about what the twelve notes represent.

The jurors remained Sphinx-like after the last note and huddled together to decide the girls' fate.

"Did you see their faces?" Zhanna whispered to Frina. "They are going to say no."

After a few agonizing minutes, the chairman of the jury rose and spoke to Dmitri.

"Mr. Arshansky, your daughters play very well. We are pleased to accept them as students, and to offer them scholarships of 200 rubles per month each."

Tears welled in Dmitri's eyes. The girls giggled. It was the first time the conservatory had awarded scholarships to children so young. But even more extraordinary was the identity of the man who would be their teacher, Professor Abram Lvovich Luntz. Among the most esteemed pedagogues of his time, Luntz never took children as students, but he was so taken by Zhanna's performance of the prelude and fugue that he told the other jury members he wanted to teach the sisters.

It was Professor Luntz who introduced Zhanna to a piece that would speak to her unlike any other, and that would become much more than another part of her repertory—Chopin's *Fantasy Impromptu*, at once brooding and melodic, stormy and serene.

Professor Luntz gave it to me one day and I started
without delay and with great curiosity to see how
hard or easy it was and I couldn't stop practicing it.
The creation is so perfect, so spontaneous that no one
who has hearing ability can miss it. Chopin's ability
to create the most gorgeous melodies in fast speed, with
quick notes, staggered me. Professor Luntz praised my
progress after a week, and I kept going like a choo-choo
to perfect the piece. When Professor Luntz approved it,
I felt that I had become a grown-up. I played Fantasy
Impromptu *in the conservatory and then everywhere*

else in concerts and private places. I knew that my love
of it would capture the listeners.

The girls had lessons three times a week with Professor Luntz to work on individual technique, but he was not their only teacher. Once a week they studied ensemble and general musicianship with pianist Regina Horowitz, whose younger brother, Vladimir, made his Carnegie Hall debut in 1928, a year after Zhanna was born, and had issued many recordings. Zhanna, who never heard a phonograph record until moving to Kharkov, would have been shocked to learn that her teacher's brother was fast becoming the most celebrated pianist in the world.

To us she was not Horowitz's sister but just another
teacher who was supposed to have a brother in America
who sent her chocolates and a gorgeous black fur coat. So
I was always looking around her studio for chocolates.

The conservatory provided priceless access for young students, a chance to see legends up close. The crème-de-la-crème of Russian and European music came to Kharkov to lecture and perform. The night that violin virtuoso David Oistrakh performed with pianist Victor Topilin, the concert hall at the conservatory was so packed that Zhanna and a few other children were seated on the stage, at the feet of the musicians.

We were only six feet away—we could almost touch
the two idols. They played Mendelssohn's Concerto in
E Minor. It was unbelievable, like heaven descended

on me. Time stopped. In the last movement there was
a joyful succession of passages that only the greatest
violinist could execute so effortlessly. Topilin sounded
very different from many pianists—unshowy,
completely substantial, with full sound no matter how
quiet he played. I lost my heart to him, too. When it
was over we screamed and jumped.

The first phonograph record Zhanna ever heard was of a brilliant young pianist, Rosa Tamarkina, just seven years older than herself. Tamarkina's recording of the 10th Rhapsody of Liszt "was like seeing electric lights for the first time." Zhanna had a new hero and role model. When she learned that Tamarkina was scheduled to play at the largest concert hall in Kharkov, Zhanna arrived early to get a seat in the front row.

Rosa had a shiny black bob and bangs, a shiny pair of
pumps, and an aquamarine silk dress. She was a vision
of someone who was preordained to do the right thing
with the creation of Chopin. She brought out the glory
of his F-minor concerto for me. Tears of happiness were
pouring out of my eyes—it stamped Chopin in my
musical heart forever.

Afterward, the star-struck Zhanna followed Tamarkina out of the concert hall and ran after her down the street.

I just wanted to keep her within my sight. I was too shy
to say anything. To me, she was an absolute goddess. I

knew my limit. I had respect. No words could express
my gratitude and admiration. She looked back at me
and smiled and kept walking.

The sisters' artistry blossomed in the rich environment of the legendary conservatory. Regina Horowitz quickly recognized that they were too advanced for the other children in her class and began instructing them in ensemble—four-hand arrangements of repertory such as Brahms Hungarian Dances and Schubert Marches. For the first time the sisters sat side by side on the piano bench, Frina's hands on the upper-register, soprano keys, Zhanna to her left on the bass register where tempo and rhythm are controlled—logical seating since Zhanna had played with her father many times while Frina had no experience in four-hand. From the start it was a felicitous partnership, their playing betraying no trace of sibling friction.

We had a very good, professional attitude toward the
music. We couldn't afford to have any kind of fuss.
That's what impressed people when they heard us—that
we loved the music so much. It was a ball for everyone
who listened.

Meanwhile, Professor Luntz was shaping them as solo artists, but his influence extended beyond the keyboard. He and his wife, Isabella, also a fine pianist, had no children, and treated the girls as their own.

The scholarship money helped put food on the Arshansky table, but there was nothing left for extras, even proper concert dresses. Before the sisters' debut in one of Kharkov's largest concert halls, Professor Luntz gave them a length of deep blue silk with a pattern of tiny snowflakes. It was crafted into matching dresses by the mother of Zhanna's good friend and neighbor, Ada, who lived on the next street. The families were very close. Ada took lessons from Dmitri, and Zhanna spent hours at Ada's apartment rehearsing on their piano while Frina was practicing at home.

The concert was a triumph, winning enthusiastic notices in the newspapers. Word spread through the musical community about the remarkable Arshanskaya sisters, now ten and eight years old, and soon they were concertizing regularly and traveling to Leningrad and Kiev to perform in music Olympiads.

The signing of the Hitler–Stalin non-aggression treaty in 1939 triggered a burst of euphoria and commercial activity that enabled Zhanna's grandparents to move to Kharkov where they took an apartment and opened a small shop selling cakes and other sweets.

Stores filled up with food we had not seen in many years. For me and Frina it was an absolute joy to have our grandparents back in our lives. We walked into their shop and knew we would get the most marvelous cakes with apples inside.

Cakes, concerts, circuses—Zhanna loved her life in Kharkov. If only she didn't have to go to school! Her first year of grade school in Kharkov was a replay of kindergarten in Berdyansk.

*Once again, I had nothing to do. I could read and write
and do multiplication very fast, while other children
were suffering over the alphabet. So I sat there wearing
myself out doing nothing—being very bored and getting
more and more conceited. As a consequence, when I
moved up to higher grades, I had absolutely no study
habits.*

Zhanna saved her deep reservoir of self-discipline for the
piano, giving the full measure of her passion and focus as she
practiced hours a day under the critical, loving gaze of her father. The sisters continued to grow as artists and celebrities, winning a local competition that earned them an opportunity to
perform at the summit of Russian music, Moscow State Conservatory, along with a few other gifted students from across the
Soviet Union. It was not their first time in the capital. The family had traveled to Moscow once before to visit Dmitri's sisters,
Betty and Fania, and on the way took a side trip to Leningrad.
Without prior notice, Dmitri went to the music conservatory
and asked that Zhanna and Frina be heard by professors. His
audacious request was granted.

*Father was very much interested to know the opinions
of specialists. I do not remember what we played, but it
was on a golden piano.*

For their prize performance in Moscow, both played Bach
and afterward were taken to a room to choose a gift. True to
their interests and personalities, Zhanna, ever the curious intel-

lectual, selected a fountain pen, while the gentle and nurturing Frina chose a doll with eyes that opened and closed.

For most of the performers that day there would be no encore, no return trip to the conservatory. The alma mater of Rachmaninoff, Scriabin, Gilels, Richter, Shostakovich, and Oistrakh admitted only a fraction of even the most gifted students. But Professor Luntz made sure that his star pupils returned to Moscow. He arranged a private audition with Professor Alexander Borisovich Goldenweiser, the Zeus among a constellation of pedagogical gods at the conservatory. He had been a classmate of Rachmaninoff's and was a frequent house guest of Leo Tolstoy, playing Chopin sonatas for the famous writer when he was confined to bed with illness. For two unknown child pianists to play for Goldenweiser was like a first-year divinity students being granted an audience with the Pope. Zhanna was keenly aware of his stature.

He had the whole world waiting to study with him.
Nobody was higher than Goldenweiser, especially to me
because he taught Rosa Tamarkina.

The family could not afford train tickets for everyone, so only Sara accompanied the girls to Moscow, where they stayed with Dmitri's sister, Betty. The audition was at Goldenweiser's apartment on the seventh floor of a building with steep staircases and no elevator—an exhausting challenge for Sara. A champion swimmer in her youth, she developed asthma and heart trouble after childbirth, and now gasped with every step. When they finally reached the seventh floor, Sara had to pause to catch her breath before knocking on Goldenweiser's door. A housekeeper ushered them into an airy room with two grand pianos and piles of books and sheet music. Goldenweiser shuffled into the room, a small, elderly man with a big head of white hair standing on end. He lowered himself into an oversize chair and motioned in the direction of the pianos. Zhanna went first.

He just said, "Go ahead." Did I really have the talent? I knew he would decide. But I was not nervous. I am never nervous playing before true musicians, only the public. It was my pleasure to play for him. I played a Bach partita. I remember how profoundly he was listening. I had never seen anything so concentrated.

Goldenweiser said nothing when Zhanna finished. He nodded at Frina to take her turn. Zhanna watched Goldenweiser as he listened to Frina. She marveled at how intensely he concentrated, as if he were a scientist peering through a microscope at the molecular structure of a diamond. Afterward, he was silent for a few moments, glancing at the girls sitting side by side on the piano bench. He turned to Sara.

"I will accept them—and they will each get a 100-ruble-a-month scholarship."

Sara and the girls could not wait to tell Dmitri. The train ride home to Kharkov seemed endless. But after a joyous celebration dinner of smoked sausages and sweets, reality intruded. Studying with Goldenweiser would mean moving to Moscow, where rents were exorbitant and job prospects for Dmitri were dim. The Arshanskys already were struggling on the 400 rubles a month the sisters received from the conservatory in Kharkov. They could not live on half that in Moscow. Staying in Kharkov was a simple matter of survival, Dmitri concluded.

The tragic irony of his decision began to take shape on September 1, 1939, when Hitler blitzkrieged Poland, only days after he signed the pact with Stalin and the weary Russian people thought they had been spared the horror of another war. Hitler's army would never reach Moscow. Kharkov, and the Arshanskys, would not be as fortunate.

Chapter Five

School 13 was on Karl Marx Prospect, a short walk along a leafy boulevard from the Arshansky home at 48 Katsarskaya. The school conveniently operated in two shifts, so one sister could be home practicing on the lone piano while the other was in class. Chronically distracted and bored by rote learning, Zhanna absorbed little new knowledge in the classroom but delighted in the "intermissions."

A drab, fortress-like edifice epitomizing Soviet architectural style, School 13 had broad, echoey staircases and tall windows that bathed the hallways in daylight. A cacophony of shouts, giggles, and whispers bounced off the walls as students gathered in little knots between classes. Zhanna was drawn to the social whirl like a moth to a porch light. Irina Vlodavsky was content to remain in the shadows.

It was an early autumn day in 1940, when they both were thirteen, that Irina first spotted Zhanna at school during a break.

"I was standing near a window and saw a girl across the corridor who impressed me with her beauty. She was standing among other pupils, but so unlike them. Zhanna was slim as a young birch tree, with big gray eyes, chestnut curls to her shoulders, and a high neck. Never in my life had I seen eyes beaming with such joy of life and friendliness. Her open-hearted nature and emotional generosity made her so different from the other girls. So naturally I got attached to her with all my heart."

Irina was shy and studious, most comfortable in the company of Tolstoy and Dostoyevsky and Pushkin, of Twain and Dreiser and Maupassant. Zhanna was a gregarious extrovert who chafed at sedentary pursuits and basked in the public spotlight. But they shared a love of music, curious intellects, and a puckish sense of humor. The odd couple soon became best friends, strolling arm in arm down the boulevards, laughing and trading girl talk. They called each other by their nicknames: Zhanna was "Zhaba"—frog, for her large, alert eyes. Irina was "Psina," a teasingly profane salute to her love of dogs. Irina would visit the Arshansky home and sit for hours on the sofa, her legs tucked under her, reading as the sisters practiced under their father's watchful eye and discerning ear.

"My own sad experience playing piano made me keenly realize their huge talent. They were floating free in the spheres of high music. It was a miraculous process, watching, listening to how the divine melodies of Chopin, Rachmaninoff, Listz, Brahms, Tchaikovsky, Beethoven and Mozart were born under the fragile, childish fingers of the girls. It spoke to my heart unlike anything else. After that, I could not hear piano music and not think of them."

Irina was at the Arshanskys' apartment the day Professor Luntz presented Sara with the length of deep blue, snow flake-printed silk to make dresses for the sisters' performance in Kharkov's largest concert hall.

"We are standing around the table, as if enchanted, watching the soft, beautiful stuff streaming under Sara Konstantinovna's thin fingers. What was she thinking about at that moment? The style of the dresses? How charming they would be in the dresses performing on a big stage? Their shining future as virtuosos? As for the concert, I remember a fully crowded hall, a huge stage with a grand piano or two in the center, and two small childish figures, as if lost in all that vastness. But as soon as they found themselves at the piano they showed an absolute command over the audience. They played duets and solo, the repertory of a highly skillful master. The reaction of the audience and the newspapers the next day was enthusiastic."

Irina marveled that the adulation never went to their heads. "They were wunderkinds, surrounded by many delighted people, but none of the noisiest success could spoil these prodigies. They never showed even a shadow of conceit. They were just the same modest, sweet little girls."

I hate conceit, simply hate it. I am always looking for other people's achievements. I would not be able to go through life worshipping so many musicians completely if I thought I was the limit, the highest thing. I thought they over estimated me.

Naturally averse to expressions of overripe sentiment, Zhanna deflected the extravagant praise with self-deprecating irony. She liked to present her friends with artistic postcards bearing breezy inscriptions which masked deeper feelings and dodged pathos. It was easy for Irina to read emotion between the lines of a card Zhanna sent her mother.

"My mother and Zhanna didn't need much time to grow to love each other. For my mother's birthday on the eve of a new year, Zhanna presented her with a postcard printed in Poland, remembering my mother's Polish roots. It was a very beautiful Christmas postcard—a prohibited topic in the Soviet Union—with a brightly decorated fir tree, angels, and Christ. On the back it said, 'Warm Congratulations' and ended jokingly, 'That is all. Zhaba, 28.12.40.' That's a feature I always loved and valued in people—not to take oneself too seriously. And here was a girl who had already felt the taste of glory."

As 1941 arrived with the Soviet Union still at peace, Zhanna and Irina were immersed in the happy, self-absorbed existence normal to thirteen-year-olds, unaware of the events outside the borders of their country and their own concerns. They lost themselves in silver-screen fantasies from America—*The Great Waltz* and *One Hundred Men and a Girl*, a musical comedy starring Deanna Durbin and the famous conductor Leopold Stokowski.

"The irresistible charm . . . the triumphant beauty and singing, the very music of the films—that unreachable, festive and distant world enchanted us," Irina said. "I can't even say how many times we ran to the cinema to be drawn into that holiday of life. For us, inexperienced teenagers brought up on ideologically controlled, fleshless films, those were unforgettable emotions."

It was not only schoolgirls bedazzled by Hollywood who were unaware of the gathering threat to their existence. Alarmingly, the adults around them weren't aware either. Since signing the non-aggression pact with Hitler in August 1939, Stalin had used his control of information and news available to Russians to perpetrate a grand illusion of peace and better times ahead. But in the spring of 1941, the illusion began to crumble as inexorably as a sand castle before the incoming tide.

Irina's family usually spent the summer at a rented dacha, or summer home, near Kiev. In April, a friend of her mother's, a military man, warned her it would be better to stay home this summer. He did not say why, but the reason soon became clear when the government began running air-raid drills. Sirens roared and delighted teenagers ran down the street with stretchers trying to persuade passers by to lie down and pretend to be dead or injured. It still seemed very much a joke to everyone. At School 13 all students were required to enter a competition—"Be Ready for Toil and Defense"—to see who was fastest to put on a gas mask. Irina detested the contest and did not covet the merit badge. To her great surprise, she won the badge and—to her embarrassment—a kiss on the forehead from their military instructor.

Despite the silly rehearsals, or maybe because of them, it all seemed like a game—until June 22, 1941, the day the final walls and turrets of Stalin's fantastic castle collapsed, and the engulfing torrent rushed in. Irina was at home on that sunny summer day.

"I was sitting on the sofa reading, my mother was sweeping the floor. Through the open windows a slight wind moved the lace curtains, and the aroma of something baked filled the flat. And then, at 12:15, the tranquility of the Sunday morning was broken by the voice of Molotov on the radio, announcing the treacherous attack by Germany against our country. My mother stood motionless with the broom in her hand. She already had been through World War I, when her family was forced to leave

Poland for Ukraine. She was sixteen at the time and worked in a military hospital. She had seen the bloody backside of war."

Not surprisingly, Zhanna at the same moment was out on the streets. She and her father had spent the morning together, happily exploring markets, gossiping with strangers, strolling through city parks brilliant with summer flowers. Now they sat at the base of the towering statue of Taras Shevchenko, the revered Ukrainian poet, savoring ice cream from a street vendor. They were jolted from their reverie by Molotov's voice blaring from the radio speakers positioned around the city for official announcements.

"Citizens of the Soviet Union!" he began. "The Soviet government and its head, Comrade Stalin, have instructed me to make the following announcement."

Zhanna and her father listened in disbelief as Molotov described the beginning of the end of their world as they knew it. Molotov's voice faded in and out of Zhanna's consciousness like a spectral presence in a nightmare sure to end at any moment, yet goes on an on.

"Today, at 4 A.M., without presenting any claims against the Soviet Union or issuing a declaration of war, German troops attacked our country. . . . This perfidious aggression against our country is treachery without precedent in the history of civilized nations. . . . The full responsibility for this robber attack on the Soviet Union falls entirely on the bloodthirsty German fascist rulers. . . . Our valiant Army and Navy and Air Force will discharge with honor their duties . . . . The whole country must now be joined and united as never before. . . . Our cause is just. . . . Victory will be ours."

Everyone in the street began to cry! The Ukrainians
already had enough misery. We ran home to tell Mother
and Frina this horrible news.

Three million German soldiers and more than three thousand tanks crossed the Soviet border that day. The ominous code name for the invasion was Operation Barbarossa, named for Frederick I Barbarossa, a German king who waged successful war on the Slavs in the twelfth century. This was not just a military operation to secure lebensraum—"living space" and rich farmland—for the German people; it was a cleansing operation to rid the land of Slavs, Jews, Bolsheviks, and all others Hitler regarded as "vermin."

On the eve of Operation Barbarossa, the Soviet "first strategic echelon"—the initial line of defense on the border—had rough parity with the German army in manpower and numerical superiority in tanks, aircraft, and artillery. What it did not have was a sound command structure and leadership at the top which fully comprehended the looming threat. On June 15, a week before the invasion, Stalin declined the request of his generals, Zhukov and Timoshenko, to send an additional fifty divisions to the border. Such a move, he said, would be provocative and signal war, which he did not believe was imminent.

"Germany is stuck in a war in the West, and I am certain Hitler will not risk creating a second front for himself. Hitler is not such a fool as to not understand that the Soviet Union is not Poland, not France, not England, not all of them put together."

The first weeks of the war showed how thoroughly Stalin had miscalculated. It was Hitler who had played *him* for the fool. Molotov's brave talk of victory now seemed like pathetic propaganda. There were no air-raid shelters, and Kharkov citizens were ordered to dig trenches and cover them with boards and sandbags. But soon the authorities ran out of boards and sandbags, leaving Irina and many others to cower in roofless "shelters" when the bombing began.

"They came every night at the same time with German punctuality. Like cockroaches we huddled in those cracks, listening anxiously to the growing roar of the German planes and the firing of our anti-aircraft guns. Our helpless openness to the dark, death-threatening sky allowed us to watch the battle above us. Enchantingly beautiful red lines of tracer bullets and long silver rays of searchlights glided about the black sky. One night the rays crossed, catching a tiny dark spot and leading it to fire from our anti-aircraft guns. A moment later we heard a distant explosion. We rejoiced."

Dmitri helped dig trenches, but there were none close to the Arshanskys' home. Every night, as the sirens howled, they walked several blocks to take shelter in the basement of a large hotel. By day, Zhanna and Frina performed for Russian soldiers stationed all around the city at events organized by the conservatory. School 13 was converted into an evacuation center to shelter refugees streaming in from western Ukraine. Classes went on in an old building nearby with the sound of explosions punctuating the teachers' lessons. Irina was unfazed by the constant percussive din. "It was not bravery, but something like childish ignorance or naivete, the feeling that you are protected by the world of adults. And for me, of course, there was a spirit of adventure and romance evoked by books."

Irina's young imagination was fired by fairy tales—Russian, German, French—the poetry of Pushkin, the tales of Turgenev and Chekhov, and by translations of Western classics such as *Tom Sawyer* and *The Adventures of Huckleberry Finn, Robinson Crusoe, Gulliver's Travels, Treasure Island,* and the "*The Last of the Mohicans.*"

"Russian children's literature lacked that wonderful spirit of adventure which was so abundant in American literature," Irina said. Still, her favorite book, the one that struck the deepest chord, was *Under the Midnight Sun* by a shadowy countryman.

"It was about a group of teenagers boating in the North Sea," Irina said. "There are adventures, hunting for spies—an obsessive topic in our country at the time—friendship, dedication and betrayal, all seasoned with nice humor. The author's name was Aurov, but I am not sure it was his real name because he perished during Stalin's terror. It was surprising the book had not been prohibited."

Such terrible truths about Stalin were unfathomable to the fourteen-year-old Irina in the fall of 1941 as the German army moved inexorably, and murderously, across Ukraine.

"We had been convinced that we lived in the best country in the world," Irina said. "Our government thoroughly protected its people from bad news. In the country of victorious socialism there couldn't be any disasters. We never heard of floods, earthquakes, or accidents. We grew up under the slogan, 'Thank you, Comrade Stalin, for our happy childhood.'"

Though shocking, the invasion of June 22 had not been enough to finally shatter Comrade Stalin's zealously cultivated illusion of socialist utopia to which Irina clung like a blanket or stuffed animal a child has slept with from birth. The great awakening, the moment her "happy childhood" ended, came the day a German bomb exploded a block away from the school.

"The children on our street ran to see what happened. A bomb had struck a multi-story house and cut it into parts. One part lay in ruins. The undamaged part stood with its interior, its guts—rooms, kitchen, toilets—open to everybody. There was something miserable, inexplicably shameful in it, as if being naked to strangers' eyes. We stood shocked. It was the first time I personally felt the shock of war."

As the German army, the Wehrmacht, swept east across Ukraine, it was followed by mobile killing units called *Einsatzgruppen,* whose only job was to kill as many Jews as possible, as quickly as possible. Its favored method, designed for maximum efficiency, was to line people up before huge trenches and shoot them in the back of the head so they would crumple directly into the ditch. On September 29, 1941, the *Einsatzgruppen* murdered nearly 34,000 Jews in two days at Babi Yar, a ravine outside Kiev, about 250 miles west of Kharkov.

The Holocaust—the systematic liquidation of Jews—had begun in earnest in the Soviet Union. And Kharkov was next.

The Wehrmacht was the blunt instrument of Operation Barbarossa, the battering ram that burst through the front door of Ukraine, laying waste and paralyzing the occupants with terror. It was then left to the *Einsatzgruppen* to carry out the Führer's ideological mission of "cleansing" the premises of Jews, a task for which they had been specially chosen and trained. The *Einsatzgruppen* were formed in May 1941 after Hitler put

SS chief Heinrich Himmler in charge of liquidating the Jews. Those recruited for the four *Einsatzgruppen* units—A, B, C, and D, ranging from 500 to 1,000 men—were not the criminal or thuggish dregs of the regular army. To the contrary, many came from officer training schools. The *Einsatzgruppe* ranks included lawyers, medical doctors, and intellectuals. Ernst Biberstein, a commander of unit C, was a Protestant pastor, theologian, and church official. These were the men chosen to execute the mass slaughter conceived by Hitler and rationalized in the demonic casuistry of Himmler in an address to SS officers.

"When somebody comes to me and says, 'I cannot dig the anti-tank ditch with women and children, it is inhuman, it would kill them,' I have to say, 'You are a murderer of your own blood because if the anti-tank ditch is not dug, German soldiers will die, and they are the sons of German mothers. Our concern, our duty, is our people and our blood. We can be indifferent to everything else. I wish the SS to adopt this attitude to the problem of all foreign non-Germanic peoples, especially the Russians."

Even before the massacre at Babi Yar, many Kharkov citizens had decided to flee east beyond Stalingrad—the Germans' destination—to safety in the Ural Mountains and Siberia. Stalin had ordered Kharkov destroyed to render it worthless to Hitler, and declared that those who stayed would be considered enemies of the state. There were also growing rumors of Nazi atrocities against Jews. Kharkov citizens had three choices: Hitler's blitzkrieg, Stalin's scorched earth, or a train east to an uncertain destination.

Joining the exodus were Ada's family, and Zhanna's cousins, Tamara and Celia, and their parents, Semyon and Eve. Semyon purchased tickets for his family and also for the Arshanskys. So did Ada's father. The night before the train was scheduled to leave, Semyon came to the Arshanskys' flat. Dmitri was in another part of the city, digging trenches. Semyon pleaded with Sara to use the tickets.

"Have you not heard the rumors?" he said. "They are slaughtering Jews. Please, Sara, for the sake of your daughters—you must go!"

Sara was unmoved. She had listened to Dmitri's stories of the German soldiers who occupied his hometown, Poltava, during World War I. They were polite, cultured people—music lovers. Zhanna and Frina learned to play on a piano imported from Germany. The girls' musical future was in Ukraine—and it was impossible to take a piano on the train!

"Why should the Germans want to kill us?" Sara said. "We have done nothing wrong."

"At least let us take the girls," Semyon pleaded. Sara took his hands and kissed them.

"Good-bye, Semyon. We will be here waiting for you after the fighting ends."

Even if Sara and Dmitri had shed their blinders and comprehended the onrushing horror, Sara was too weakened by her asthma and heart condition for the rigors of an evacuation, as Zhanna had discovered on a reconnaissance mission.

I went to the train station where people were evacuating. They fought any way they could to get on the train. Some hung on with one arm. I could not imagine my mother doing this. So we stayed. We just

hoped we would be left alone in our flat, with almost
nothing. We never dreamed we would be killed. We
thought it was an entirely temporary state of affairs.
The Germans would send us to a work camp, they
would be kicked out, and we would be home again.

Irina, too, was fleeing east. Her mother, a nurse, was a volunteer at the hospital—actually the Hotel Krasnya, which was converted into a hospital facility—and as the Germans closed in on Kharkov, plans were made to evacuate all hospital workers and their families. They would travel to Siberia on cattle cars which had been crudely adapted for people. The "bathroom" in each car was a bucket in a corner curtained by a sheet. Irina's train was scheduled to leave September 19, but the evacuees were warned to board days early because the train might leave at any time. Some were not able to board until the final desperate moments before the train pulled away from the station. Celia, Tamara, and their mother were pulled through a window into the train by Semyon as ticketless hordes surged around the cars and clamored for a seat on the departing train. With numerous delays, their journey east to a refuge would take an excruciating thirty-five days.

On September 15, Zhanna went to the station to say goodbye to her best friend. They embraced tearfully, saying little. Zhanna handed Irina a final postcard. On the front was a drawing of two musicians in Polish costumes, one playing a woodwind instrument, the other a violin. Irina thought she saw in the image a subconscious urge to hide anxiety and fear, "as if the hands stretched at parting in vain to stop the moment, to keep from vanishing, in spite of everything, our happy childhood."

On the back of the card, in Russian, Zhanna addressed a message to "Inooha," one of her nicknames for Irina.

"Well, Ino, if you ever forget me, then watch out! Wishing you happiness in everything you do. So long from me forever. Please never forget me. Love, Zhaba and Puzha (the sisters' nicknames). Kharkov—15.09.41."

Irina could never forget. Their music was imprinted on her soul for eternity. In a small red box she placed Zhanna's postcards and a photo of the sisters—"one sitting, another standing, leaning slightly on the back of a chair. The sitting one was a beauty, the other one, standing, was the embodiment of childish charm." And in Irina's mind she kept an image which could never be lost or become faded by time.

"In my memory there appears a picture of three girls walking along Goncharov Boulevard. One is tall and slim with chestnut curls streaming in the wind, another one a bit smaller with short thick plaits, and the third one, Frina, the youngest, with short golden curls and a few freckles on a pretty face. Silently and attentively, she listens to the girlish talk her senior girlfriends are twittering about. We are walking to my house. . . . "

Chapter Six

Forsaken by Stalin and now besieged by Hitler, Kharkov had become a sad and dangerous place, pockmarked by Luftwaffe bombing and scorched by Stalin's wrath. It felt shrouded in doom. The streets were no place for a fourteen-year-old, even a bold and restlessly adventurous one. For the first time in her life, Zhanna was a prisoner in her own home. When the German Sixth Army, fresh from its brutal conquest of Kiev, rolled into the city on October 23, she heard about it from neighbors. They spoke of atrocities which taxed the limits of her imagination.

One morning not long after the Germans arrived, Zhanna tentatively opened the front door of the apartment and glanced up and down Katsarskaya. At the far end of the street she saw proof of the neighbors' incredible tales: a body hanging from a lamppost. Another from a tree.

This was the Nazis' modus operandi after entering a city—to terrorize the population into docility with public hangings, from trees, lampposts, balconies. On Dzerzhinsky Square, the towering monument to Taras Shevchenko, national poet of Ukraine, had been desecrated. The iconic bronze figures of farmers, workers and soldiers arrayed on pedestals beneath the poet were festooned with corpses.

Zhanna was filled with revulsion, like some horrible bile rising up in her throat from the pit of her stomach. For all her fearlessness, the girl named for Joan of Arc had a near-phobic aversion to violence in any form. Once, when she was three years old, her parents took her to a silent movie at the only theater in Berdyansk. It was an American movie, a slapstick comedy featuring a short fat man and a tall thin one. When they began to trade comical blows on the head, little Zhanna did not see the humor.

I began to scream uncontrollably. There were no guns or knives, but there was a fight. I thought the men were hurting each other and I couldn't take it. I was screaming loud enough to cover the sounds from the screen and hiding myself in my father's lap. We had to leave.

The Sixth Army made Kharkov its headquarters and established a military government which issued regular decrees to the city's captive population of nearly half a million. Nazi intentions toward the Jews of Kharkov were immediately apparent. The daily bread ration was 5.25 ounces. For the Jews, 2 ounces. Most of those arrested in daily roundups were Jews who—out of necessity or naivete—had not fled the city. Among them was Irina's Uncle Pinja.

"He was a common white-collar worker—energetic, goodhearted and friendly. As soon as the war began, his two sons Ben and Ika entered the army and went to the front to fight. Unfortunately, my uncle shared the illusions about a 'cultured nation' and stayed in Kharkov with his wife, Minna. He was taken as a hostage and hanged on the balcony of his own flat."

The Arshanskys stayed inside the apartment and awaited their fate. Normal life came to a halt. The sisters did not dare play the piano for fear of drawing attention from German soldiers patrolling the streets. Dmitri kept repeating his belief that they were going to a work camp in Poltava. It was torture for Zhanna.

There was nothing but fear and hiding and killings and investigations. Nothing. We were just hoping that somehow we would be left alone in our miserable existence.

And for a short time they were. Perhaps Dmitri was correct. Just possibly they would be forgotten or ignored by the Germans. Then late one night, the quiet of the apartment was shattered by a thumping knock on the door. A jolt of clarity shot through Dmitri. This was not the knock of a friend or neighbor. And of the seven families in the building, the Arshanskys were the only Jews. Anyone could have betrayed them. It was all over.

Dmitri opened the door to a lone Nazi officer. He spoke only German and some broken Russian, not Yiddish like the friendly German soldiers Dmitri remembered from World War I. Barging into the room without comment, the officer did a quick visual inventory of the family and its meager belongings. Smirking, he turned to Dmitri.

"Gold?"

Dmitri shrugged his shoulders and held out his empty palms.

"Lying Jew!" the officer snapped. "What else do you have?"

We had nothing except for the piano, which he could not take by himself, and my father's violin. He spotted the violin and we caught our breath. We begged him not to take it. In our horror he opened the case just long enough to see that it was not empty and snatched it. It was a knife in our hearts. The violin was like a member of the family. It was played and heard every day, and it was happy. He took it in the same spirit they took gold from the fillings of dead Jews. But he could not take its vibrations that came from our existence. The vibrations would remain, without the body.

Dmitri hoped the officer was satisfied with his precious plunder, that it would be enough to buy freedom for his family from any more terror. A few nights later that hope, too, was dashed. The banging on the door was even louder than before. Two more Germans, just foot soldiers this time, had come for their spoils of war. Seeing nothing else of value, they lifted the piano but could not maneuver it out the door and became enraged. One of them grabbed Dmitri and held his hands behind his back, while the other slammed Sara against a wall and put his pistol to her head.

"Show us your hidden treasures or I will kill her!" he screamed, looking back at Dmitri.

"But we have nothing—just pots and pans!"

Zhanna and Frina cowered in the corner, crying hysterically.

"Filthy, lying Jew! Give me your money or I will kill her!"

The thugs finally left empty-handed. Sara and Dmitri were unhurt, but everything had changed.

That was the beginning of true terror. After my father's violin was gone and they attacked our mother, we knew anything could happen to us.

Dmitri's illusions about the Germans were shattered. His dream of one day watching his daughters take their place in the brilliant firmament of Russian music was forgotten. Now he simply hoped they could survive. The revulsion over Nazi atrocities gave way to rage directed at the man who could have prevented or at least mitigated the nightmare.

The horror we encountered after the German occupation would have been unimaginable if Stalin had warned us. We relied on him to say, "Look, Jews, you better get out of here!" Without his secrecy, most Jews would have survived. Our leader, our father, our brother— Josef Vissarionovich Stalin—became Hitler's silent collaborator in the east.

The certainty of the impending horror became clearer when the Nazis began a systematic count of all Jews in Kharkov. Some clutched to the notion that the Germans were making a list of people to be used for slave labor. But most knew better. A few wealthy Jews were able to bribe officials and send their children away. The rest turned to desperate measures. Sara heard a rumor that proof of baptism would shield the girls from Nazi persecution.

My mother started walking long distances every day to find a priest who would change us into Christians. I wouldn't let her walk by herself on awful roads, or no roads at all, so I went with her. But Kharkov was a ghost city and all of our walking ended in nothing. The one Russian Orthodox priest we got to see refused to do the baptism.

The Jews of Kharkov did not know it—there was no official announcement—but their fate was sealed on November 26 with the arrival of *Sonderkommando 4a*, sub-unit of *Einsatzgruppe C* responsible for "cleansing" operations in central Ukraine. The commander was Paul Blobel, who had directed the massacre at Babi Yar. Soon after his arrival in the city, the murder of Jews increased. Usually they were taken to the Hotel International and tortured before being killed, most in *gazwagens*—ordinary delivery trucks converted into rolling gas chambers. The Russians called them dushegubki—"killers of souls." A hole was cut in the floor and a pipe inserted which fed the truck's exhaust fumes into the cabin packed with Jews. Sometimes a driver impatient to be done with the task would press the accelerator all the way to the floor.

"As a result the persons to be executed die of suffocation and do not doze off as was planned," an SS doctor reported. "If my instructions are followed, and the levers are properly adjusted, death comes faster and the prisoners fall asleep peacefully. Distorted faces and excretions, such as were observed before, no longer occur."

The gazwagen murders were just a rehearsal for the final liquidation of Kharkov's Jews. On December 14, with the census complete, the Nazi command distributed leaflets ordering all Jews to prepare for immediate evacuation to an abandoned tractor factory outside the city. They were told that those who failed to comply with the order would be shot on the spot. They were not told that those who *did* comply also would be shot—just at different spot.

We knew it could mean only two things: they would make us laborers in a concentration camp, or it meant the end of our lives.

There was snow on the ground and more on the way. Dmitri sold the family's dishes, lamps, and rugs to buy a sled to carry clothing and bedding. There was no one to buy the piano, and no way to take it with them—wherever they were going. Zhanna wept at the thought of the piano falling into the hands of the who Nazi brutes that threw her mother against the wall and held a gun to her head.

December 15 dawned cold and bright, a thin blanket of snow creating an ironic tableau of serene beauty. Thousands of Jews headed to collection points, bundled in heavy coats and clutching a few possessions. Sara packed a bit of food, mostly dried fish and bread. The Arshanskys were headed down Kat-sarskaya in a throng of evacuees when Zhanna suddenly stopped in her tracks.

"I must go back!" she said, turning on her heel. "I forgot something."

"Zhanna!" her mother cried.

"Don't worry—I will catch up with you!"

Zhanna sprinted the four blocks back to their apartment. It already seemed to have acquired an air of desolation. Zhanna stood for a moment at the center of the room, once a place of ceaseless activity, now a still life of the family's final desperate moments there. She went to the piano and began riffling through a stack of sheet music. Bach, Schumann, Handel, Debussy . . . here it was! The piece she loved above all others—Chopin's *Fantasy Impromptu*. Professor Luntz had introduced her to the piece and given her the sheet music with a gravure portrait of a dashingly handsome young Chopin on the front. She grabbed the music, tucked it inside her shirt, then raced out the door and never looked back.

The six Arshanskys—Zhanna, Frina, and their parents and grandparents—walked together in the mass of 16,000 Jews that formed a giant gray sea flowing along Moscow Avenue toward the factory twelve miles away. By noon the snow was melting in the sunshine. Dmitri and Sara struggled to pull the sled over patches of mud and rock.

The most painful thing was not the hunger, not the cold,
not the fear. It was the way we were disgraced by the
Germans. They were laughing at us while we marched,

taking photographs to send home to proudly show future
generations how they led unarmed people in freezing
conditions to their extermination.

The street was lined with Ukrainians, non-Jews, most of them silently observing the march. Occasionally a woman would push her small children out of line toward the crowd in the hope they would be taken by a sympathetic bystander. If a Nazi guard noticed the subterfuge, the mother was shot.

By no means were most bystanders sympathetic. The Nazi invasion had reignited an ancient, virulent strain of Ukrainian anti-Semitism which had lain dormant since the wave of pogroms from 1917 to 1921 which claimed more than 100,000 Jewish lives. Though Jews had borne a disproportionate brunt of Stalin's political purges and forced collectivization in the 1930s, official expressions of anti-Semitism, in word and deed, had been temporarily sacrificed to the greater need for national solidarity against the fascist invaders. Stalin's long-running campaign against the Russian Orthodox Church had been suspended for the same reason.

The Nazi invasion blew the already loose lid off the Pandora's box of Ukrainian anti-Semitism, which by 1941 had metastasized into a more lethal cancer compounded of ancient hatred plus the now widely accepted canard that Bolshevism was a Jewish conspiracy. Nazi propagandists assiduously fueled the notion of "Judaeo-Bolshevism" through the use of Ukrainian newspapers, radio stations, public exhibitions, even movie theaters, which offered films such as *The Jews and NKVD* and *Stalin and the Jews.*

The pent-up furies ripe for exploitation by the Nazis can be seen in a resolution adopted in April 1941 by the Second General Congress of the Organization of Ukrainian Nationalists (OUN). It declared, "The Jews in the USSR constitute the most dedicated support for the ruling Bolshevik regime and the vanguard of Muscovite imperialism in Ukraine. The Organization of Ukrainian Nationalists combats Jews as supporters of the Muscovite-Bolshevik regime and at the same time makes the popular masses conscious of the fact that the principal foe is Moscow."

While fanning the embers of old hatred for the Jews, the Nazis were planting in Ukrainians a fresh loathing built on fear for their own lives. After entering a town or city, the Germans would post a warning: "Should anyone give asylum to a Jew or let him stay overnight, he as well as the members of his household will be shot by a firing squad immediately."

The potent cocktail of fear and hatred concocted by the Nazis had the intended effect. Some 24,000 Jews died in pogroms in western Ukraine in the early stages of Operation Barbarossa at the hands of "intoxicated" Ukrainians driven to a blind homicidal rage by the noxious Nazi cocktail. The invaders were pleased to stand by and watch the rampage. The son of the chief rabbi of Lvov described a scenario that would be repeated countless times across Ukraine.

"Immediately after the entry of German troops, anti-Jewish riots started in which many thousands of Jewish inhabitants of Lvov lost their lives. The pogrom was organized by the Germans, but the atrocities were committed by the Polish and Ukrainian mobs."

As the Nazis went about the business of liquidating Jews in the Ukraine they had the assistance of the "popular masses," as the OUN called them, and even better, Ukrainian auxiliary police who became their willing, often enthusiastic, accomplices. And the Germans desperately needed accomplices. The Jewish population in the Ukraine at the start of the war was approximately 2.5 million. The two *Einsatzgruppen* units assigned to the region totaled about 1,400 men. Fortunately for the outnumbered *Einsatzgruppen,* they could count on the Ukrainian police—*Schutzmannschaften*—to be their surrogates in the slaughter.

Most Ukrainians did not engage in pogroms, and a good number risked their lives by harboring Jews. But many still welcomed the Germans with "bread and salt" as their liberators from Stalinist tyranny, and openly celebrated the forced exodus of Jews in hopes it would bring them continuing German protection from Stalin. They used discarded Torahs to stoke fires and turned the pages of the finest Torahs into playing cards to be sold at markets. Some rushed out to rob the defenseless Jews of their remaining meager possessions, as Zhanna witnessed on the interminable march out of Kharkov.

The throng of doomed souls crept along Moscow Avenue under a thin cloud of frozen breath, silent except for the sound of boots crunching snow and a muffled cry or half-stifled curse. Some collapsed and died of exhaustion, and their bodies were pushed to the side of the road. Winter days are short in Ukraine, and as night fell the marchers were stranded in the countryside, still miles from the factory, without shelter from the Arctic wind.

In the growing darkness and confusion, the grandparents had become separated from the rest of the family. Dmitri searched in the pitch-blackness, but it was futile. They were gone. His thoughts turned to surviving the night. Wandering into a nearby field, he found a wooden shed the size of an outhouse. It had no door but was better than no shelter at all.

The wind hit us, but not as hard. Only three of us could fit inside, in a standing position, so all night we took turns, one of us standing outside. After walking all day, the fatigue in our legs was overpowering—they could hardly hold up our bodies. We did not know if our mother could survive the night.

Sara made it through the hellish night, but many marchers who found no shelter did not. Morning light revealed corpses all along the road and in the fields on either side. The march to the factory resumed under light guard. The Germans knew that the Jews had no weapons and no place to run.

Daylight brought a moment of joy amid the horror for the Arshanskys.

"Look!" Zhanna shouted, pointing at two shuffling figures among the thousands streaming onto the factory grounds. "It's Grandma and Grandpa!"

Miraculously, they survived the night and finished the march to the makeshift ghetto that would be the condemned Jews' home for the next two weeks. Not all the Kharkov Jews were there. Some, including a group of 400 children, infirm, and old people, were not capable of making the journey.

Ever efficient, the Nazis took them to a synagogue on Mesh-chansky Street, locked the doors from the outside, and left them to die from cold and starvation. They may have been luckier than the ones who reached the tractor factory.

Chapter Seven

The barracks at the abandoned, tractor factory outside Kharkov consisted of 27 identical rectangles arranged in long rows, each building designed to house 60 to 70 workers, a capacity of roughly 1,800. The Nazis deemed it adequate for temporary storage of 13,000 Jews.

They kept telling the Jews they were headed for a labor camp, and most believed it because to believe anything else was unbearable. They believed it even though the living conditions were more suited to cattle being led to slaughter than to future workers. The barracks had broken windows, leaky roofs and cement floors. There was no heat or running water, the stoves did not work, and there were no bathrooms. The captives were given no food and had to stand in long lines for a cup of water. The compound was enclosed by barbed wire and guarded by SS soldiers. It was a ghetto.

From the first day, people began dying from exposure—the winter of 1941 was brutal even by Russian standards—and from starvation and disease. Some simply went mad. An SS officer enticed a starving two-year-old boy with candy, bending to offer the treat. As the child reached for it, the officer grabbed his neck with both hands, strangled him, and threw the boy's dead body at his mother's feet. Hysterical, she began to kiss the soldier's hands. He took out his pistol and shot her in the head.

The Nazi guards shot prisoners at random, casually, as if they were rats in a garden. People were shot for not surrendering warm clothing, watches, and other valuables. They were shot for *not* having valuables. One man was shot when he left his barrack at night to scoop up a handful of snow for his feverish baby. Every morning the newly dead were hauled from the barracks and thrown into nearby anti-tank ditches.

Large groups of the old and sick were loaded on trucks and taken away—no one knew where. Gazwagens were used inside the ghetto when it was not convenient to take the doomed prisoners into the woods or an open field and shoot them.

Those in the ghetto who were allowed to live were stripped of their dignity. The women's "toilet" was a shed with three holes in the ground, overflowing with waste from diarrhea and other gastrointestinal disease caused by the filthy brown liquid that passed for drinking water on the grounds.

It was inhuman. All I could do was run away. The sight of women the age of my mother and grandmother made me shake in shame for the Germans. It was a disgrace to their high education and culture. I wanted to put those who created this hell in the same place where I saw these women suffering for no cause. That's where I wanted Hitler and Himmler and Goebbels.

Wiping away tears of outrage, Zhanna reconnoitered the

grounds in search of some privacy. She found a small fenced area behind a building that appeared to be a dumping ground for trash and garbage.

The fence was a little shorter than I was, but I didn't see any reason I could not use it for my bathroom. The only problem was that the Germans probably would shoot me if they saw me. Since fear was present every minute anyway, I decided to take the chance.

More people were dying every day from starvation. Their bodies were dumped in a "living grave" in the ghetto where the moans of the nearly-dead rose up from the corpses. The Arshanskys were down to the last bits of the dried fish Sara had packed. Zhanna knew what had to be done. She had to sneak out of the ghetto, go back to Kharkov and find food for her family.

My parents couldn't stop me. It was impossible to hold me. I was like a pet returning to his home. I had to see what was happening on my street. I had to bring back food.

Zhanna's solitary explorations starting at age three in Berdyansk had prepared her well for the clandestine journey. At dusk, before the ghetto's bright searchlights were turned on, she slipped out of the barrack and crept along the barbed wire until she found a gap she could squeeze through. It was nine miles to Kharkov, and Zhanna had only a thin coat and no food. After walking for two hours, she was too cold and hungry to go on. She spotted a small house up ahead with a faint light in the window. Would they dare open the door to a stranger in the dark? Were they kind-hearted gentiles—or anti-Semites who would report her to the Nazis? It was a chance she had to take. She knocked on the door.

> *They opened the doors for me and asked no questions.*
> *They just saw a cold kid. I said I am walking to*
> *Kharkov and I have no place to sleep. They allowed me*
> *in, gave me something warm to eat, and put me in bed*
> *with themselves.*

When Zhanna reached Kharkov the next day, she realized she had no plan for finding food. She had no money and the market stalls were mostly bare anyway. Then she remembered that her mother used to dig ham skins and potato peels from the garbage of German soldiers stationed at the end of Katsarskaya Street near their apartment. Wary of being recognized by a schoolmate or by one of the many people who knew her and Frina as musical celebrities before the war, Zhanna waited till dark to return to Katsarskaya and fill her pockets with German garbage.

It was not much, but enough to keep her family alive as hundreds around them perished. The ghetto festered with death. What one prisoner saw was true in barrack after barrack.

"Here was hell. Dead people, dishes, down from pillows, clothes, food, fecal matter—everything was mixed. In one corner was a dead woman lying on the bed, her hands dangling down, and a little baby was sucking her dead finger. In the other corner was the dead body of an old man."

The German soldiers were given a day off to celebrate Christmas, and they searched prisoners for any hidden sweets or valuables to fill their party tables. The day after Christmas, the Jews were ordered to relinquish all their belongings in preparation for transport. But to where? For weeks they had been told they were destined for a labor camp in Poltava or some other point south. But Dmitri, who knew the area well, was suspicious. He noticed babies and very young children being loaded on trucks which then left the ghetto and headed north, not south to Poltava.

When he saw the trucks go north, my father knew they were going to kill us because there was nothing to the north. It was the road to nowhere.

Sara could see the dead end ahead. She saw her children's lives slipping away. She had to do something. Oblivious to the armed guards, she left the ghetto and started walking in the direction of Kharkov—in search of what, she did not say.

She started to run and was gone for hours. It was her being, her soul that ran—her legs could hardly move. We thought she would end up dead. She had a heart condition and asthma and was so exhausted. I said to Father, "Where did Mother go?" He said, "She went to find something for you." She came back with nothing.

As stealthy as she was, Zhanna figured the guards must have seen her sneaking in and out of the ghetto, and her mother had walked by them in broad daylight. She always wondered why the guards didn't bother to shoot them. Now, as the Arshanskys prepared to leave the ghetto, the answer dawned on her.

The guards knew what was coming—they knew where we were headed. It's so much easier to end many lives in one operation where the ditches are ready than to bother with separate persons. It was not worth the bullets, or the noise, to shoot just one Jew.

Chapter Eight

D mitri was correct—the road north was to nowhere. It went to Drobitsky Yar.

Yar is the Russian word for ravine, or ditch. Places with natural ravines are ideal for mass murder because less digging is required to bury the corpses. Three months earlier, the Nazis had murdered nearly 34,000 people, mostly Jews, at Babi Yar outside Kiev. The Drobitsky ravines, only a short death march from the ghetto, provided the Nazis a convenient dumping ground for the Kharkov Jews.

Like most people around the world in January 1942, the Jews in the ghetto knew nothing about Babi Yar, and they could not know what awaited them at Drobitsky Yar: two giant pits, one 320 feet long, the other 180 feet.

At Babi Yar, in a breathtaking display of ferocity and Teutonic efficiency, the Nazis murdered 33,700 Jews in two days, about 700 an hour. Most were machine-gunned in the back, though some were killed with a single bullet to the back of the head. Col. Paul Blobel, the commander who directed the slaughter, was given the Iron Cross, Germany's highest award for valor.

The Nazis did not have enough soldiers to replicate that valorous efficiency at Drobitsky Yar, and had to be content with eliminating the Kharkov Jews over several days. The Arshanskys were among the last group of prisoners to make the trek north from the factory ghetto.

None of the Jews knew what lay ahead, but Zhanna's sixth sense detected an ominous change in the air. The evacuation from Kharkov had been rather listless, the mass of doomed humanity moving slowly and formlessly toward the ghetto. Zhanna noticed a greater sense of urgency and order as the Germans herded the Jews for this march.

> *They got everybody organized into true columns and rows. Every row consisted of six people. Our family made one row. On the far right was my mother, then Frina and me, my father next to me on the left, then Grandma and Grandpa.*

The rows formed a series of long columns, each about the length of a city block. Separating the columns were rumbling transport trucks carrying German soldiers and equipment. Ukrainian guards with rifles walked alongside the columns, shadowed by SS officers with holstered pistols and rubber whips they occasionally cracked to speed up the marchers.

It was another bright and bitterly cold day. The sky was pale blue and the undulating fields of Drobitsky were cloaked in the pure white of a virgin snow. Zhanna noticed that it sparkled like diamonds in the sun. She fixed the image in her mind, and wondered how such things could happen on a day so beautiful.

To Dmitri the march had an air of finality. He felt in the pit of his stomach that they were being taken to a place from which none of them would return. Walking next to Zhanna, he ached with guilt and self-loathing. What a fool he had been to trust the Germans! How he wished he had listened to his brother-in-law Semyon and taken his family east to safety. How he longed to hear his daughters play, one last time.

"Raus!" snapped a jackbooted SS officer, cracking his whip at the faltering marchers.

A Ukrainian guard was walking alongside, in step with the Arshanskys. With Zhanna listening, Dmitri turned and began speaking quietly to the guard in Ukrainian. "Look at me—you can see that I am not a Jew. Please just turn your eyes away and let my little girl go."

Dmitri pointed to Zhanna. He knew that she could survive on her own—she had done it since she was three when she explored Berdyansk alone. Frina was only two years younger, but she was slower to mature and was never a creature of the streets like Zhanna. Dmitri could not send her into the wilderness. And two girls running out of line risked creating a commotion that could result in neither making it. But for Zhanna alone, there was hope.

The Ukrainian guard marched ahead in silence, unmoved by Dmitri's plea. Perhaps he could buy Zhanna's freedom, Dmitri thought. But with what? He had no money, nothing of value. But wait! His pocket watch. He had managed to hide it deep in his coat when the Nazis were stripping the Jews of their valuables at the ghetto. It had a white porcelain face, Roman numerals, and a gold cover. Zhanna never saw her father without the watch, in his vest or on his belt. Dmitri had offered it many times as a bribe in the days when he was being arrested and jailed regularly by Stalin's secret police. The henchmen always rejected it, demanding gold that Dmitri didn't have. Perhaps fate had protected the watch for this life-and-death barter.

Dmitri fished the watch from his coat and furtively flashed it at the guard. The young Ukrainian, not much older than Zhanna, took the watch and slipped it into one of his pockets. "Any time she wants to run," he told Dmitri, "let her go and I will pretend not to see."

Father and daughter traded looks. No words were needed. They understood each other so well. The plan was in place. But with Ukrainian guards and SS patrolling columns, Zhanna could not just bolt out of line. She needed an opening, a distraction. Up ahead she saw two babushkas standing on the side of the road, watching the procession. Next to them on the ground were two large rings of barbed wire, slightly unraveled and ragged.

This was my chance! I would jump out of the column and pretend to be an observer tangled up in the wires, trying to untie myself. I looked around and didn't see a guard and knew I had to jump.

There was no time for parting hugs or even muffled good-byes with her family, just fleeting glances that spoke of a lifetime together. Dmitri removed his heavy winter coat and placed it over his daughter's slight shoulders. It was very long and stretched nearly to the ground. Then Dmitri whispered his final words to Zhanna.

"I don't care what you do, just live. Go!"

Zhanna leaped from the line, and in that awful moment something magical happened.

I could feel the eyes and good wishes of many souls on their last march. It was like they were holding me up in the air above the danger, so I would not be harmed. I felt their passion and knew it would never die. Our hearts were connected.

In the concealing bulk of her father's coat, Zhanna grappled with the barbed wire and tried to blend into the dreary landscape.

I became one of the gray women, just watching the column. I saw a German looking straight at me—he had a whip—and I thought he would stop and grab me, but he kept going. I saw my mother and father looking back at me. I stood and watched that column a long time, as if my legs were buried in the ground, and cried and cried and cried.

Chapter Nine

S hivering in the coat haunted by her father's scent, Zhanna stood by the side of the road and watched as the last column of Jews headed for Drobitsky Yar grew smaller and fainter and finally dissolved into nothingness on the horizon.

Zhanna was utterly alone. She knew instinctively what awaited Mama, Papa, Frina, and her grandparents at the end of the road to nowhere. But she could not afford to think about that now. Her job—the reason Papa bribed the guard—was to survive. And it seemed that all her years of solitary explorations had been a rehearsal for this terrible day.

I did not hesitate. I realized I had to turn around and go the opposite direction from where the Germans were leading the columns. I knew which way to go to Kharkov. I was a professional already. I began walking and thought, "This is it."

She walked south for hours across bleak landscape, her father's coat dragging on the ground, the memory of their last moments together throbbing like a fresh wound. I must stop crying, she thought. The tears were stinging her cheeks in the sub-zero cold. By nightfall, Zhanna was only halfway to Kharkov. Her clothes were frozen to her body by urine—the treeless fields offered no cover for a makeshift bathroom—and she was light-headed from hunger.

As Zhanna forged on in the frigid darkness, she was propelled by the rush of an emotion she had suppressed in the horror and grief of losing her home and then her family. It was anger—a deep, toxic anger that welled up from the depths of her soul like molten lava and made her cheeks burn. She remembered how the Nazis had stopped to piously celebrate Christmas—using the condemned Jews as servants to prepare their party tables—before starting the death march to Drobitsky Yar the next day.

Such cowards, these mighty Hitlerite Christians, carrying out the murders as far away from witnesses as they could manage! If the Jews are such vermin and the Germans are doing the planet a favor by getting rid of us, why make it such a secret? Maybe they aren't sure Jesus Christ would approve? Poor Jesus—he had the most forgiving heart, but nothing is limitless.

Zhanna was on the same road she had traveled on her surreptitious mission to Kharkov while in the ghetto. She was nearing the home that offered sanctuary the first time. She agonized. With Nazis on the lookout for any stray Jews, was it fair to ask the same family to repeat its risky generosity? She did not even know their names. But Zhanna had no choice. And once again the door opened, no questions asked, and she was welcomed under the covers of a crowded bed.

Zhanna was going back to Kharkov because she had nowhere else to go. She expected no welcome mats. The Nazi-occupied city bore little resemblance to the vibrant cultural mecca where she grew up making friends and music. It was now a shattered place where death was the price for harboring a Jew, and behind many doors were Ukrainian anti-Semites eager to betray a Jew to the Nazi occupiers in exchange for bread or material goods. Going door to door in search of refuge would be Zhanna's personal game of Russian roulette. The peril she faced was evident in an *Einsatzgruppe* status report to Berlin.

"The Jews have disappeared from Kharkov. Nevertheless, there are still some Jews in hiding in the rural districts as well as in town. This elimination of the Jews has occurred with the help of the Ukrainians who, after adequate indoctrination, have recognized the destructive nature of the Jews. They have reported Jews in hiding, or families who housed them. These are being arrested each day. With a few exceptions, the attitude of the population of Kharkov to the Jews is absolutely negative."

Jews who escaped into the forest were hunted down by the Germans with the help of Ukrainian collaborators and peasant informers fearful for their own lives. Zhanna had become a fugitive from injustice in her own land.

Soon after reaching Kharkov, she spotted a familiar face on the street, Professor Polevsky, a piano professor at the conservatory. Zhanna knew his wife, a cello professor, and his daughter, Zoya, a fine cellist who had a collection of shoes and clothes

Zhanna envied. Only months ago, she would have shouted out merrily to the professor and asked about Zoya. Now, she just watched in silence as he crossed the street in front of her.

He couldn't recognize me because I had my father's coat thrown over my shoulders. I wanted so much to greet him—but I was afraid to scare him.

Bored German soldiers patrolled the streets and leaned against the doors of boarded-up shops for a smoke. Zhanna avoided eye contact and walked briskly toward Katsarskaya, her old street, and the home of Svetlana Gaponovitch, a close friend from School 13. Her father was a Jewish doctor, but he had moved away. Svetlana was sure to welcome her with open arms, Zhanna thought. She knocked on the door and waited. Then she knocked again. Finally, the door edged open far enough for Zhanna to see Svetlana and her mother staring out.

"Svetlana! It's Zhanna—Zhanna from school!"

"We know," said Svetlana's mother. "Go!"

"But Mrs. Gaponovitch—"

"Get away!" she said, and the door closed.

Zhanna was shocked. So this is what it is like to be a leper, she thought. A leper without a colony. It was growing late and cold. Where could she go? Zhanna thought of another girl who lived on the street, Lida Slipko. She was a classmate but not a close friend. Her mother was an illiterate woman from a small village and was rumored to be an anti-Semite. It probably was a waste of time to knock on their door, but Zhanna had nothing to lose.

*They opened the door and took me in immediately. They
had so much humor—I loved them both. Human beings
are capable of stunning compassion.*

Zhanna was learning that war made strange and unexpected
bedfellows. Lida and her mother were wonderful, but Zhanna
knew she had to keep moving. But where could she go next?
Who would open their door to an official pariah?

"There is Nicolai Bogancha," Lida said. "I have heard that
his mother and father are good-hearted people. And they have
room for you."

Zhanna's pulse quickened. Nicolai! It was a name she had not
considered. She had long admired Nicolai and his home from a
distance. He was a brilliant student but painfully shy with girls.
They had exchanged little more than glances and hellos in the
hallway. His well-to-do family lived in a large house behind a
forbidding gate at 32 Katsarskaya, a short walk but a world apart
from the Arshanskys' flat at 48 Katsarskaya.

*The gate was so high that I never got to see what was
inside and I was never invited in. I was dying to know
what was inside, because Nicolai was my favorite boy.*

The solid, double-doored wooden gate stood ten feet high,
with pillars on either side, and was painted a drab gray-green. It
did not cry out for visitors. Mustering all her considerable gump-
tion, Zhanna rapped sharply on the gate. Within moments, one
of the doors swung open.

I saw the loveliest and most welcoming figure saying
to me, "I know who you are," stretching her arm out
to touch mine and pulling me inside. I had never seen
Nicolai's mother before, but her lovely smile told me
who she was. I was so excited to see inside the high
fence, and even more excited to see my studious and shy
classmate. "Hello, Zhanna," he said, and started some
interesting conversation. My eyes were full of tears. I
am not a religious person but I kept thinking, "Thank
God for the Boganchas.

The Boganchas had managed to protect their inherited
wealth from Stalin's disastrous economic policies. They could
afford to have food brought to them from villages, and had
delicacies such as chocolate which most Russians could only ad-
mire in store windows. After weeks of deprivation and terror,
Zhanna felt as if she had entered a Garden of Eden.

How did I end up in the most desirable place while
running away from the very worst prospect? I was
melting from this gift of fate.

But Zhanna and the Boganchas knew that she could not stay.
Too many people had seen her. Svetlana and her mother, who
closed the door in her face. Lida and her mother, her first saviors
in Kharkov. Perhaps even Professor Polevsky had spotted Zhanna
out of the corner of his eye, but was afraid to acknowledge her.

"We will keep you," Nicolai's mother said the first day, "but it
is impossible for anyone to know because we will all be killed."

It was also impossible to keep Zhanna's presence a secret. She was too well-known because of her music. Sooner or later, word would leak out that she was back in town and the Gestapo would come banging at the Boganchas' gate. She could not allow that to happen. She began to contemplate the unthinkable—leaving Kharkov.

Zhanna had been with the Boganchas for a few days when Nicolai arrived home one afternoon with an excited look on his face.

"Zhanna, there is a rumor on the street that Frina is alive. She is here in Kharkov."

The blood drained from Zhanna's face. She stared disbelieving at Nicolai.

"But that is impossible."

"They say she was taken in by a family not far from here who found her sitting on the doorstep."

Zhanna put her head in her hands and sobbed with joy. She could not imagine how the little sister she always considered so dependent, the baby of the family, had survived. Did the same Ukrainian guard who let her go also allow Frina to flee? Did she reach Drobitsky Yar and see her parents and grandparents murdered, and somehow escape? It did not matter—she was alive!

When the Boganchas learned that Frina was staying in a nearby apartment on Katsarskaya, they insisted she come and join Zhanna in their home, thus doubling their own jeopardy.

They did it without being asked, even though they knew that Jews and those hiding them were being shot. They were true heroes.

When they were reunited in the Boganchas' living room, the sisters embraced and cried together. But Frina said nothing about her ordeal—how she escaped, what she witnessed—or about the fate of Mama, Papa, and the grandparents, and Zhanna didn't ask—that day, or ever. Some things are unspeakable.

As the girls were contemplating and dreading their inevitable departure from Kharkov, Nicolai's parents were thinking about it with the benefit of adult foresight. If they were to survive the war, it would not be as Zhanna and Frina Arshanskaya. They would need whole new identities as non-Jews. With the Boganchas' creative help, Zhanna and Frina became Anna and Marina Morozova, orphaned daughters of an officer in the Russian army who was killed in action. Their mother died in the bombing of Kharkov.

They chose Anna and Marina because they were easy names to remember, and Morozova because it carried a reminder of the season and happier times. Moroz is Russian for frost. "Dyed Moroz" is Grandpa Frost, the Russian Santa Claus. With new names came new birthdays. The girls would need I.D. papers and the only way to get them was through an orphanage. No child over fourteen could be admitted to an orphanage, and Zhanna would be turning fifteen soon, on April 1. "Anna" needed a birthday much later in the year. Zhanna chose December 25. Frina—"Marina"—changed hers from April 10 to December 20, so the two birthdays would still be close together, and therefore easier to remember.

The idea that we were going to be calling each other by different names was unbelievable to us. We practiced

day and night. We learned to lie about our parents'
names, our life story—everything was false.

For sentimental and practical reasons the sisters decided to go west to Poltava. It was their father's beloved hometown and it was in the opposite direction of the German army as is headed east to Stalingrad. The Boganchas arranged for a horse cart to take the girls to the outskirts of Kharkov. From there, they would walk fifteen miles to Lubotin to catch a train for Poltava. Beyond that there was no plan, except to stay alive.

Thanks to a gold watch, the kindness of strangers, and strength bequeathed to them by their parents, Zhanna and Frina had eluded the pits of Drobitsky Yar. But there were many more ravines in Ukraine, with Nazis eager to fill them with dead Jews. The long and perilous journey of Anna and Marina Morozova was just beginning.

Chapter Ten

AT THE OUTSKIRTS OF EACH TOWN WAS A DITCH WHERE
A SQUAD OF EINSATZ MEN WAITED FOR THEIR VICTIMS.
WHOLE FAMILIES WERE ARRAYED, KNEELING OR STAND-
ING NEAR THE PIT, TO FACE A DEADLY HAIL OF FIRE.
—OPENING STATEMENT OF PROSECUTION AT NUREMBERG
TRIAL OF EINSATZGRUPPE COMMANDERS

After being reunited at the Bogancha home, the sisters never spoke of the death march or their escape, not to each other, not to anyone. Nor did they speak of their parents and grandparents, whose fate at Drobitsky Yar was, mercifully, unimaginable to them. Indeed, the scale and the methods of the Nazi mass murder in the Ukraine were beyond the ken of normal adults, much less children. Between the invasion of the Soviet Union in June 1941 and the end of December, the Nazis slaughtered nearly a million Jews, either one at a time with a bullet in the head or dozens at a time with machine gun fire in the back. Sociopathic behavior was standard operating procedure for *Einsatzgruppen*, the mobile death squads whose sole function was to kill as many Jews as possible in the shortest period of time. They literally took no prisoners, regardless of age or circumstance or feebleness of mind or body. A court judgment detailed *Einsatzgruppe* execution of patients in a mental asylum.

"The barrel of the pistol was placed between the two ligaments under the scruff of the neck, facing upwards. The shot was supposed to come out at the forehead so that the bullet would have traveled through the entire length of the brain. If that succeeded, blood and brains splashed out of the pulsating wound and death occurred instantly. After the shot was fired, the patients were pushed into the creek and carried away by the strong current. Their bodies disappeared in the subterranean creek."

By 1941 the persecution, killing, and ghettoization of Jews in Germany and Poland was widespread. But it was in Ukraine that Hitler's hatred of Jews—a malignant seed which had been germinating for years, watered by growing quantities of Jewish blood and misery—mated with his loathing of Slavs and flowered darkly into systematic mass murder. Construction of the Auschwitz II-Birkenau extermination camp had not even begun in September 1941 when *Einsatzgruppen* murdered 34,000 Jews in two days at Babi Yar outside Kiev. The gas chambers and crematoria at Birkenau did not claim their first victims until spring 1942. The killing of Jews at Treblinka commenced that summer. By that time, the elimination of Jews from Ukraine was nearly complete.

The Jewish population of Ukraine prior to the Nazi invasion was about 2.5 million. It is estimated that 850,000 Jews escaped the Nazi dragnet by evacuating east to the Ural Mountains and Siberia. The combination of extermination and evacuation proved to be a lethally effective cleansing agent. Russian war correspondent Vasily Grossman provided an eyewitness account of the results in his article "Ukraine Without Jews."

"There are no Jews in Ukraine. Nowhere—Poltava, Kharkov, Kremenchug, Borispol, Yagotin—in none of the cities, hundreds of towns, or thousands of villages will you see the black, tear-filled eyes of little girls; you will not hear the sad voice of an old woman; you will not see the dark face of a hungry baby. All is silence. Everything is still. A whole people have been brutally murdered."

There were reasons the *Einsatzgruppe* mission in Ukraine became a whirlwind of unexpected fury and magnitude. Stalin's failure to prepare for war left the country virtually defenseless, allowing the Wehrmacht to advance east at astonishing speed—350 miles in the first ten days. Cities fell like dominoes to the German army, clearing the stage for *Einsatzgruppen* to perform their "cleansing" duties. Stalin made their job easier by producing a sea of unwitting victims. Out of deference to Hitler, his ostensible ally after signing the non-aggression pact in 1939, Stalin blocked news of Nazi atrocities in Poland and Germany, so Jews in western Ukraine had no inkling of Hitler's intentions when the Germans appeared on their doorsteps. To compound this fact, many welcomed the invaders in the hope they would free them from the yoke of Stalinist oppression. Others like Dmitri Arshansky remembered the civilized behavior of occupying German troops in World War I, and revered German culture. They were inclined to believe Nazi rumors that

Jews would be transported to labor camps, as reflected in this report to Berlin from the *Einsatzgruppe* unit that followed the Germany army into Kiev.

"The Jewish population was invited by poster to present themselves for resettlement. Although initially we had only counted on 5,000 to 6,000 Jews reporting, more than 30,000 Jews appeared. By a remarkably efficient piece of organization, they were led to believe in the resettlement story until shortly before their execution."

The Germans took Kiev on September 19. Ten days later, Iryna Khoroshunova, a resident of Kiev, wrote in her diary.

"There are terrifying rumors coming from the Lukianivka Cemetery. But they are impossible to believe. They say the Jews are being shot. Some say they are being shot with machine guns. Others say that sixteen train cars have been prepared and they will be sent away. Only one thing seems clear: all their documents, things, and food are confiscated. Then they are chased into Babi Yar and there . . . I don't know. There is something terrible, horrible going on, something inconceivable, which cannot be grasped or explained."

Three days later, after the *Einsatzgruppen* had completed the massacre of 34,000 Jews at Babi Yar, Iryna added to her diary.

"Everybody is saying now that the Jews are being murdered. No, they have been murdered already. All of them, without exception—old people, women, and children. No trains left Lukianivka. People saw cars loaded with warm shawls and other things driving away from the cemetery. German 'efficiency.' They already sorted the loot!"

Because of the suddenness and rapidity of the Nazi invasion, the Jews of Kiev and other places in western Ukraine never had a chance. The Jewish population in the east at least was given a running start—if it chose to take it. Rumors of atrocities in the west and deteriorating living conditions in the city convinced many Kharkov Jews to flee. The Arshanskys were not among them. Dmitri, especially, clung stubbornly to the belief that the reports of Nazi genocide were wrong, and the government did nothing to disabuse him of his fatal delusion. Zhanna blamed Stalin for being an accomplice to the genocide.

> *No one was told about what was awaiting us. All we had were vague rumors. Had the Soviet government wanted to save Jewish lives they would have shouted to us to run, and showed it with special transportation to leave no Jews behind. Stalin was guilty, a complete criminal not to alert Jews to slaughters in the west. If Stalin had said one word confirming the rumors, we would have crawled to get out.*

Instead, they ended up on the road to Drobitsky Yar. Miraculously, since Zhanna and Frina escaped the death march, they also escaped any sure knowledge of what happened when their parents and grandparents reached the ravine where *Einsatz* men with guns waited in trucks. Dmitri, Sara, and the rest were ordered to strip to their underwear in the biting cold, then herded by club-wielding soldiers to the bottom of the ravine, where they fell in a storm of machine gun and rifle fire. Some mothers suffocated their small children in their coats rather then send them into the pits.

The Germans did not try to hide the evidence of their crimes, or even block access to the killing field itself. Anastasya Zakharovna Osmachko, a non-Jewish resident of the nearby village of Rogan, described her visit to the ravine.

"When I learned of the murder of Soviet citizens by Germans in the valley of Drobitsky on the morning of January 7, I went to see what was happening there with my son, Vladimir, age twelve, and another eleven people from the village. In the valley we discovered a pit several tens of meters long, ten meters wide, and several meters deep. Many bodies of those who had been shot were piled up in the pit. When we had looked at the bodies we decided to go home. But we had not had time to leave the valley when three trucks arrived carrying German soldiers. The soldiers stopped us. They took us to the pit and began to shoot at us with a machine gun. When my son fell, I fainted and fell into the pit. When I recovered, I found myself lying on dead bodies. Later I heard the cries of women and children whom the Germans were bringing to the pit and shooting. Their bodies fell into the pit where I lay.

"I was in the pit from the morning until four or five in the afternoon and saw how, throughout the day, the Germans kept bringing groups of people to the pit and killing them. Before my eyes several thousand people were shot. When the Germans had finished the slaughter they left the place. From among the corpses, groans and cries went up from the living wounded. About a half an hour after the German soldiers left, I crawled out of the pit and ran home. My son and the other people who had come with me had been shot."

Zhanna knew instinctively her family's terrible fate at Drobitsky Yar, but did not speak of it or allow her imagination to give it form. The unarticulated knowledge remained locked in a dark recess of her soul—sacred, profane, untouchable. Only by suppressing the horror could Zhanna push forward as Anna Morozova to fulfill her father's parting plea . . . *just live!*

Chapter Eleven

The horse-drawn wagon bumped along a road rutted by winter and war, carrying Zhanna and Frina away from the protective cocoon of their Kharkov neighborhood, past familiar shops and parks and School 13, beyond the conservatory and concert halls where their precocious artistry had made them darlings of the city's musical community. It all seemed to belong to a fantastic dream now, slowly receding from view and memory as they rode in silence, their legs dangling from the back of the wagon.

Reaching inside her coat to make sure the sheet music for *Fantasy Impromptu* was still safely tucked under her shirt, Zhanna was jolted out of her reverie and back to reality. They were orphans, fourteen and twelve, left to fend for themselves behind enemy lines in the dead of the Russian winter. They needed each other to survive, but in many ways were unlikely travel partners. Except for playing piano duets, the sisters had spent little time together. Zhanna was born to the streets. Frina preferred to stay home and play with her dolls and do handicrafts with her mother.

While Zhanna was blessed with robust health and vitality, Frina's childhood was shadowed by pain and illness. In the first grade, she caught scarlet fever and doctors couldn't get her temperature down for more than a month. Then, just as Frina was getting well, the fever spawned a vicious middle-ear infection.

She was near death so much. The doctors did surgery, terrible surgery. They cut out a piece of bone behind her ear. It left her with unequal hearing and balance in her ears. The recovery lasted for months. I don't know how she survived all that—it was terrifying.

Remarkably, the illness and surgery left Frina undiminished as an artist. Zhanna believed no one played Mozart more beautifully.

Frina played the D-minor Concerto with fluent technique, but that's not why everyone cried when she played it. She grasped the spirit of the piece, the style, at barely ten years old. Her ear was already developed to a mature state, although the rest of her was a child who played with dolls every free moment. I didn't feel two years older. I felt twenty years older.

The wagon reached the outskirts of Kharkov just after noon and the sisters hopped out. They now faced a fifteen-mile walk to the train station in Lubotin, a challenging trek for trained, well-equipped soldiers, much less two young girls with little warm clothing, no boots, and just a few scraps of stale bread.

They walked for hours and met no one. There was no landscape, just a disorienting blanket of white, unmarked but for two thin lines of train track, stretching to the horizon. Night was falling. Zhanna felt stirrings of panic.

> *We didn't know where we were. We were just alone in a large, silent field. There was nothing but snow with the very red, sinking sun above it.*

Suddenly, Frina stopped in her tracks.

"What's wrong?" Zhanna asked.

Saying nothing, Frina lay down in the snow, deliberately and with ceremonious care, as if she were making snow angels.

"I am not going any more," she said, staring up at Zhanna. "I just want to be left alone."

"You cannot do that!" Zhanna said, her voice resounding in the stillness. "The sun is going down and it's getting colder. You will freeze, and I will be left alone. You have to get up! If you don't get up, I will lie down, too."

Frina lay motionless, peaceful, in the snow. Zhanna searched her sister's eyes and saw only fear, exhaustion, and resignation.

"You *must* get up," she said. "If you will not do it for me, then do it for Mama and Papa."

"I am too tired," Frina said.

Zhanna stood helplessly over her recumbent sister as the horizon faded from crimson to steel grey. The same thing in Frina's spirit which helped her to abide the terrible ear surgery and to survive the march to Drobitsky Yar would not allow this open field to become her anonymous grave. After a while she arose from her lonely respite in the snow, brushed off her white coat, and the sisters resumed walking in silence.

*It's amazing that we knew where to go in the snow. It
was pitch-black. We were not dogs—we could not sniff.
And even dogs can't find anything in the snow. We
couldn't believe it when we finally heard train noises
and saw some lights.*

The train station at Lubotin glimmered like a lighthouse,
guiding the lost travelers to safety, but it did not provide even
a temporary port in the storm. There was no place in the tiny
station for the exhausted girls to lie down. They would have to
try to find shelter in Lubotin itself, just a village with one short
block and a few homes.

*We only had to knock on one door. We were asked in
and were allowed to sleep on the stone floor in the entry
room. There was barely enough room to stretch our legs,
but we slept like the stones under us. The family was
heroic for letting us in. If the Germans had found us
there, they would have killed these good souls.*

The sisters—Anna and Marina to their hosts—rose before
dawn to leave for the station where they hoped to sneak onto
a train bound for Poltava. They had no money, but even if they
had, it would have been too risky to buy tickets without identification papers. They reached the station to find the locomotive
steaming and people boarding passenger cars. Through the window of a car near the front they saw a conductor chatting with
two German soldiers. Ducking out of sight, the girls scampered
to the back of the train and found a place where they wouldn't

draw attention: an empty cattle car. It had no heat or toilet, but there was straw on the floor, and it was better than walking through the snow.

For a long time the train didn't move. Zhanna wondered if it was really going anywhere. If so, where? And when? She was going a little stir crazy, and she needed a bathroom. Cattle are lucky, she thought. They are too dumb to know if they are moving, or to care. The train finally pulled out of Lubotin around noon and rumbled slowly toward Poltava. Through the wide-spaced iron bars of the cattle car the sisters watched the rural desolation roll by, a slow-motion frieze of ramshackle cottages, feral dogs, bent-over babushkas carrying wood, and the occasional German motorcycle left to rust in the snow. It was dark when the train rolled to a merciful stop in Poltava.

Zhanna and Frina were hungry, thirsty, and desperate for a bathroom. The large Poltava station was a sea of displaced people in transit from other places, protecting bundles of possessions they had gathered for their sudden exoduses. This is where they would spend the night before venturing into Poltava the next day. They were lucky to find room on a crowded bench, both of them squeezing into a space intended for one person. But after twelve hours of solitary confinement in the cattle car they welcomed the chance to rub shoulders, literally, with their country-men. And it would help take their minds off food—or so they thought.

On a bench across from them an old woman delicately unfolded a cloth, removed a morsel of food, and fed it to a tiny, shivering dog sitting in her lap. Zhanna's attention then turned to a man nearby who was taking off his boots. His feet were heavily wrapped in rags for warmth, much like the "foot-cloths" common among prisoners in the gulags. Perhaps he had been in the camps. Zhanna watched the man carefully unwrap each foot, clean between the toes, then rewrap the foot in the dirty rags. She was riveted.

I couldn't take my eyes off him. I needed to study his technique of wrapping. The man's concentration was fantastic. It was interesting and educational, and it distracted me from the nagging hunger in my stomach.

After putting his boots back on, the man reached into a bag and pulled out a hunk of black bread. He tore off a piece and smilingly offered it to the sisters, extending a grimy hand in friendship. Zhanna went from riveted to revolted.

I was a very fastidious person by nature. My mother was the cleanest person in the world. All I could think of was his hands and what they had been handling.

She didn't think about it for long.

We were out of bread. We were out of everything. Our hands moved toward the bread automatically. It was very dark and very good. It was gone instantly. We didn't get sick and we never forgot the man with the dirty feet. That bread would carry us for hours to come.

Chapter Twelve

"MY NAME IS ANNA MOROZOVA. I AM FROM KHARKOV.
MY SISTER MARINA AND I ARE ORPHANS. OUR FATHER
WAS AN OFFICER IN THE RUSSIAN ARMY AND WAS KILLED
IN ACTION. OUR MOTHER DIED IN THE BOMBING OF
KHARKOV."

Zhanna rehearsed her new life story over and over in her head as she sat on the hard wooden bench in the Poltava train station waiting for morning to come. Today the story would get its first true test. Up to now the sisters had managed to avoid direct contact with the enemy, but that would not be possible in Poltava.

Situated ninety miles west of Kharkov on the road to Kiev, Poltava is where Dmitri Arshansky grew up after his family moved from Mariupol when he was a boy. The region's political history is a checkerboard of influences—Lithuanian, Polish, Cossack—dating back nearly a thousand years. Built on the high west bank of the Vorskla River, Poltava is a beautiful town with fountains and parks and tree-lined boulevards, rich in culture and commerce. The leafy ambience belies its honored place in Russian history as the site of a transforming military victory. In 1709, the Russian army commanded by Peter the Great destroyed an invading Swedish force of 30,000 men, ending the Great Northern War and marking Sweden's decline as a great power and Russia's emergence. "Beaten like a Swede at Poltava" became a mocking simile in Russian for humiliating defeat.

It was on the streets of Poltava that young Dmitri befriended Yiddish-speaking German soldiers who benignly occupied Poltava in World War I—friendships which blinded him a generation later to signs of a predatory German force. Now in the grip of Hitler's army, Poltava was a perilous place for Jews.

The sisters hoped to find an orphanage in Poltava that would help them get identity papers with their new names and birthdays so they wouldn't have to live in the shadows, fearful of being stopped by Nazis on the lookout for stray Jews. But to get from the train station to the center of Poltava they had to cross a bridge over the Vorskla that was closely guarded by German soldiers checking I.D. papers.

We were absolutely terrified. We had no papers, so we had to try our story about Anna and Marina. We had practiced it many times, but this was the first real performance. My heart was in my feet.

It was just before dawn. As the girls approached the bridge they tried to cover their faces by turning up the collars of their coats. No one else was crossing the bridge, no crowd of farmers or horse carts to blend into. Their only ally was the grainy early-morning light. One of the two soldiers blocking access to the bridge stepped forward. His rifle was slung over his back.

"My name is Anna Morozova," Zhanna began in Russian. "I am from Kharkov. . . ."

The German waved his hands for Zhanna to stop. Her story had hit a language barrier. The guard walked up close enough for Zhanna to notice the brass buttons on his coat, to smell the damp leather of his boots. He reached out and moved the collars away to see their faces clearly. He looked first at Frina—more stereotypically "Russian" in appearance than Jewish with her blonde curls and freckles—then glanced at Zhanna.

"Das sind kinder!"—these are children—he shouted to the other guard. "Gehen!"—go—he said to the girls.

So we crossed the bridge. It was like crossing a stage. We were lucky—we could have been finished right there.

After the train ride from Lubotin and a sleepless night in the Poltava station, the sisters were too tired and hungry to start looking for an orphanage. They needed food and sleep. How many doors would they have to knock on this time? The supply of guardian angels is not limitless. Zhanna wondered if they had used up their share in Kharkov and Lubotin.

The courage of the Russian people is astounding. The very first door we knocked on, the people said, "Come in." There was a mother and father and two little girls. It was a lovely place with lots of light and glass—much cleaner than we were. We sat down and told our false story and they gave us pancakes, milk, and tea.

There was a piano in the home, the first one the sisters had seen since the terrible day a month before—a month that seemed like two lifetimes—when they were rousted from their Kharkov apartment for the death march to Drobitsky Yar. The parents noticed that Zhanna was staring at the piano.

"We hope that our two girls will someday learn to play," the mother said. "Do you play?"

"Yes," Zhanna said, "I can play."

The mother was skeptical. "Okay, then—play," she said, motioning Zhanna toward the piano.

And she did—Chopin's Waltz No. 14 in Eminor, from memory. The parents were stunned. The two little girls' mouths hung open.

"I want you to teach my children!" the excited father said. "You must stay here and give them lessons."

Piano lessons in exchange for room and board—a cozy arrangement, but it couldn't last. After two days of playing in-house teacher, Zhanna told the disappointed parents she had to look elsewhere for a paying job. She didn't tell them the real reason for leaving was to continue their urgent pursuit of I.D. papers for "Anna" and "Marina." She needed to find someone in authority, and venturing into the occupied town would be risky. Zhanna decided Frina should stay with the family while she scouted things out.

Zhanna relished being back on the streets, her natural habitat. Making her way into town along the wide boulevards, she recognized some of the landmarks her father had told her about—the Golden Eagle monument to Russia's victory over King Karl of Sweden in 1709, statues of the writer Nikolai

Gogol, and poet Ivan Kotlyarevsky. She began to understand why her father loved the town so much.

It dawned on Zhanna that there was only one authority in Poltava now—she must go straight to the source. She found the German headquarters in a large, ornate building with Greek columns, wide steps—and a red, black, and white Nazi flag hanging unfurled from a balcony above the entrance. Guards were posted on either side of the doors.

They ignored me, so I walked right in. There was a rotunda with beautiful floors. I climbed the stairs and entered a large entry hall with tall windows. Standing there was a man in a fur hat and the most gorgeous Russian coat that went down below his knees. He was dressed completely differently from everyone, like a nobleman from an old Tsarist family. He was cleanshaven with a pronounced nose and an expression of intelligence.

The impressive figure just stared at Zhanna with a bemused look, as if a giraffe had wandered into the building.

"What are *you* doing here?" he asked.

"My name is Anna Morozova. I am from Kharkov. My sister Marina and I are orphans. Our father was an officer in the Russian army who was killed in action. Our mother died in the bombing of Kharkov. I need some information."

The man looked incredulous. "What?" he said in Russian. "Why are you asking *me*?"

Zhanna's heart leaped at the sound of Russian. He was a countryman! Surely he would help.

"My sister and I need jobs. We have no money and no place to live."

This urchin was asking him for a job? What nerve!

"And what can you do?"

"I can play piano," Zhanna said.

The man burst out in laughter. "That remains to be seen, Anna. But first you need a place to stay. For now, you can stay at my home. *Nyanya* is alone all day when I am at work. You can give her a little help and stay until we decide what to do with you."

Zhanna thought a man of such regal bearing, with a magnificent fur coat, would live in grand surroundings. Zhanna was startled when they reached his home, a modest one-story house with low ceilings, a wood-burning stove and no indoor toilet. His bedroom had a small desk and was lined with bookshelves from floor to ceiling. This was the home of an intellectual, Zhanna thought, not an aristocrat.

Over tea and cookies, Zhanna's mysterious host told his story. His name was Oleg Stepanovich. He was a professor fluent in several languages. His wife died in a prison in Siberia and he now lived with *Nyanya,* his nanny from childhood. His job at German headquarters was translator and right-hand man for the Nazi commandant who ran Poltava. This is a powerful man, Zhanna thought. He is in a position to help us, or to betray us.

Oleg showed Zhanna to her "bedroom"—a cramped space in the passageway between the kitchen and his room. There was a cot big enough for only one person.

"What about my sister?" Zhanna said.

"There is not space here for two people," he said. "I will try to arrange a place for her to stay."

Oleg found a family that seemed like a dream match for

Frina. Both parents were teachers, and they had two children and a nice home. But so did the evil stepmother in Cinderella.

They were heartless and cruel. They kept Frina starving and working like a slave. I saved little pieces of bread to take her. But I didn't see how I could complain after Oleg went to so much trouble. It broke my heart because my place was terrific.

Oleg didn't express them, but he had gnawing doubts about Zhanna and her story. Something about it, about *her,* did not ring true.

"You talk about playing the piano," he said to her one day.

"I have been playing since I was five," Zhanna said. "Before the war I was given a scholarship to the Moscow Conservatory, but it was not possible for my family to move there."

"Well then, I must hear you play," Oleg said. "Let me take you to a theater where there is a piano."

Oleg sat alone in a sea of empty seats. On the unlit stage, Zhanna opened the keyboard cover on the baby grand and turned to her audience.

"What would you like to hear?"

"It is your choice—*you* are the performer," Oleg said with just a hint of mockery in his voice.

Zhanna played for twenty minutes, an extemporaneous program of Bach and Chopin. When she finished, the audience of one gave her a standing ovation.

"No doubt, Anna—you can play," Oleg said, thoroughly startled by what he had just heard.

"Thank you very much," Zhanna said.

And so Oleg's suspicions were allayed, but only for a short time. After the sisters had been in Poltava four about two months, there was an influx of refugees from Kharkov, non-Jews who had stayed after the Germans invaded but found that life in the gutted city had become intolerable.

I was walking down the street in Poltava and saw people I knew from the conservatory in Kharkov. They ran up and threw their arms around me and screamed, "My God! You are alive!" I was petrified. I was trying to get away from people who knew us. There was nothing we feared more.

The Kharkov people would make it difficult for Zhanna and Frina to stay in Poltava under cover. Then something happened that made it impossible. One day Frina was visiting Zhanna at Oleg's home. They were in Zhanna's little space, trading idle chatter, when Zhanna let her guard slip.

"Frina. . . ."

On the other side of the thin walls, Oleg looked up from his book. Frina? He waited until Frina left and then confronted Zhanna.

"I heard you speaking with your sister," he said. "Who is Frina? You must tell me your true story, Anna—or whoever you are."

Zhanna, not a crier, dissolved in tears—from embarrassment at lying to this wonderful man, and from fear of what was to come. She steadied herself and told him the whole story.

"It's impossible for you to stay here," he said. "If the Germans find out who you are, and they will, they will not spare you."

He said they would be safer in Kremenchug, a small town about seventy-five miles southwest of Poltava on the Dnieper River, farther from the front lines. Oleg paid a farmer to take the sisters to Kremenchug in a wagon. Zhanna had wondered if a man in his position would betray her and Frina, or help them. She had her answer.

His one ambition was to save us from these murderous foreigners. He may have answered to the Nazis, but his heart belonged to his countrymen.

It seemed that Zhanna and Frina still had not used up their share of guardian angels.

Chapter Thirteen

Zhanna and Frina still did not have identity papers for "Anna" and "Marina" as they prepared to leave Poltava for Kremenchug in mid-April 1942. Living in a war zone without I.D. papers, especially for two runaway Jews, was living on borrowed time.

Only children in an orphanage who were fourteen or younger could be issued new identity papers. Time was running out. Zhanna already had turned fifteen on April 1. The first order of business in Kremenchug must be to find the orphanage. The professor devised a strategy for the girls.

"Here is what you do. Tell people that you are orphans looking for your Aunt Morozova who lives in Kremenchug."

"But we have no Aunt Morozova," Zhanna said.

"Exactly!" said professor. "They will say they do not know your Aunt Morozova, and will direct you to the orphanage."

Having a plan gave the girls a sense of security that made the 75-mile trip to Kremenchug in the back of a farmer's cart more bearable. They shared the space with burlap bags of produce and clothing and two scrawny chickens in a small cage. The only sustenance along the way was some bread and goat's milk, still warm from a villager's goat.

The cart reached Kremenchug in mid-afternoon as the early-spring shadows began to lengthen. The town was occupied by the Germans, but Zhanna noticed there was no destruction, at least not yet. She hoped it would be possible, using the professor's strategy, to find the orphanage before dark.

There was no one on the street to ask, so the sisters approached the first house they saw. Zhanna knocked on the front gate. Getting no response, she tried rapping on a window. After a few moments a window slowly swung open and a woman peered out. She was stony-faced.

"What do you want?"

"My name is Anna Morozova. I am from Kharkov. My sister Marina and I are orphans. Our father was an officer in the Red Army and was killed in action. Our mother died in the bombing of Kharkov. We are looking for our Aunt Morozova who lives here."

Zhanna then waited for the mute stare and upturned palms certain to meet her bogus inquiry. Instead, a look of recognition crossed the woman's face, then a smile. Zhanna was puzzled.

"Manya Morozova was here but not anymore—she died," the woman said. Then her voice grew excited. "Please wait! I am coming out! What an honor it is to meet dear Manya's nieces!"

Manya's nieces? Zhanna's blood ran cold. Morozova was a fairly common name in Russia, but what were the odds that one had lived on this very street—millions to one? What would the professor think of his fool proof plan now?

Zhanna turned to Frina. "Oh, my God. What are we going to do?"

The situation was even worse than Zhanna imagined. It

wasn't just this one woman who knew Aunt Morozova. It seems *everyone* on the street had known her, and loved her. More doors and windows opened to the commotion on the street, and soon the girls were surrounded by friends of Aunt Morozova eager to meet her nieces from Kharkov.

Before we knew it, they had started a lively remembrance session about their beloved neighbor. We hoped they would continue talking among themselves because we knew nothing about this woman who was supposed to be our aunt.

Zhanna could not avoid being dragged onto memory lane for her remembrances, which she made up as she went along. "She saw me only once, when I was a baby," Zhanna told her rapt circle of listeners. "So I do not remember Aunt Morozova. But our mother always told us wonderful things about her sister."

"Her sister?" said one of the listeners. "I thought Manya had only brothers. She never told us about a sister."

Oh, my god.

"Perhaps because they feuded for some years," Zhanna said quickly. "Mother said they loved each very much despite the problems. You know how it is with sibling rivalries!"

Zhanna's stomach was churning, her ears were hot. Somehow, she and Frina had to escape these unwitting well-wishers before they were exposed as impostors.

"It has been wonderful to meet so many of Aunt Morozova's good friends," she said. "But Marina and I must keep going. We hope to reach the orphanage before dark."

There was a chorus of protest.

"It is out of the question! We will not allow Manya Morozova's nieces to go to an orphanage! You will stay with us—for as long as you like."

Maybe it's possible to have too *many* guardian angels, Zhanna sighed. They were trapped—prisoners of kindness. Their "cell" was an apartment they shared with two young policemen.

They were marvelous young men, the first to offer us room in their apartment. We had such fun together— two kids and two cops.

There were two other apartments in the building. One was occupied by a young woman, a pharmacist. In the third apartment, larger and much nicer than the others, lived a well-educated older couple with a beautiful piano, which the girls were invited to use any time. It was a lovely refuge—clean and safe, and the policemen treated them like princesses. But they needed to get I.D. papers. And they knew that sooner or later there would be more questions about Aunt Morozova, questions they could not answer, and the charade would be exposed. They had to leave—the only question was when.

The answer came one day when Zhanna decided to visit the older couple's apartment. As he often did, the husband sat listening as Zhanna noodled at the grand piano. In a grandfatherly tone he insisted that Zhanna come sit on his lap.

His wife wasn't home—it didn't feel right. Suddenly he started to paw me. It was very nasty. I got scared and

*ran away. I knew at that moment that we must go to
the orphanage—immediately.*

Zhanna didn't tell Frina or anyone else about the groping, a crude reminder of how, at age fifteen, her body was changing in ways that posed new dangers. But early the next morning she left Frina at the apartment and set out to find the orphanage. It was on the other side of town on an unpaved, muddy road flanked by fields planted with vegetables, mostly cucumbers. The two-story wooden building was in dire need of fresh paint and a handyman.

Zhanna took a deep breath and entered an outer office where she found a man sitting behind a desk, bent over paperwork. Zhanna cleared her throat and he looked up.

"My name is Anna Morozova," she said. "I am from Kharkov. My sister Marina and I are orphans. Both our parents were killed in the war. We are looking for a place to stay."

"I am the director," he said. "We have only little children here and not much food—mostly cucumbers. We go through the Germans' garbage for bits of meat and gristle. You will be very hungry here."

"But you have a bed?" Zhanna said.

"Yes," he said, "we have a bed for you and one for your sister."

Zhanna was relieved that the director was so incurious about their background. He didn't even ask her age. It was too late to walk back to the apartment to get Frina. The director took Zhanna to a dimly lit room on the second floor and showed her the beds. She lay down and quickly fell asleep. Daylight shed a harsh light on her new home.

There were no drapes on the windows, no trees outside
to block the sun. Light flooded the room. I looked down
at the sheet—it was gray with crawling lice. I felt a
sickness all over. I grabbed the sheet and ran downstairs
to the yard to shake it out. I was shaking all over. I
wanted to burn the sheet but I could not. There were no
other sheets.

And no other choice. They must go to the orphanage, Zhanna thought, as she made the long walk back to get Frina. They must go even though Frina, so meticulously clean, just like their mother, would be horrified by the lice. The cops, the pharmacist, Aunt Morozova's many friends—they all pleaded with the girls not to go. Zhanna explained it was necessary for getting identity papers. She did not tell them about being groped by the neighbor. As the girls walked away from the apartment Zhanna looked back and saw him waving and smiling with all the others.

So we went back to the orphanage and they put us up,
and we had cucumbers, really bad, rotten cucumbers,
and we saw little children, tiny babies, crying from
hunger. All they had was cucumbers and milk without
any life in it, mostly water. They were dying from
dysentery. We would go through the German garbage
and find a piece of pork and suck on it. We felt lucky.

It was not long before the sisters got the news they had been so anxiously awaiting: the children in the orphanage would be taken to town as a group to get identity papers. They felt a huge weight lifting from their shoulders. But the relief was short-lived.

Zhanna came back from town one day with a terrifying rumor.

"The Nazis can identify Jews through blood tests," she told Frina. "The officials issuing identity papers will take our blood and learn the truth."

Was the rumor true? Zhanna could not ask the orphanage director—it would raise his suspicions, and he might send them away, not wanting the presence of two Jews to endanger the other children. Who could she ask? Zhanna thought of all the people they had met in Kremenchug. The two policemen, their buddies, were too close to high authority. Aunt Morozova's friends would not know the answer to such a question. There was only one possibility—Tatiana, the young pharmacist next door to them at the apartment. She was friendly and had medical knowledge. It meant confiding in a relative stranger, but Zhanna felt she had no choice.

Death would come anyway if the blood tests showed we were Jewish, so what was the risk? I was counting on her humanity.

Zhanna made the long walk to the apothecary where Tatiana worked. She paused to look in the window, and for a moment she was just a child again, standing in the doorway of the apothecary in Berdyansk, transfixed by the wondrous array of bottles and containers. But Zhanna had no time for reveries today. She entered the shop and went to the back where she saw Tatiana working.

"Do you remember me? I am Anna, from the apartment."

"Yes, of course!" said Tatiana. "We all miss you and Marina very much. Why are you here? Are you ill?"

"No," Zhanna said, "but I need some information."

They stepped outside in the alley for privacy and Zhanna told Tatiana her real name and the story of her escape. Then she asked about the blood.

"That's nonsense—a big lie!" Tatiana said. "They cannot identify any blood as being Jewish. Stick with your plan. I promise I will never give away your secret."

On the appointed day, Zhanna and Frina reported to the documents office prepared to give their blood and bogus biographies. The authorities did not demand blood after all. But Zhanna was still nervous. Fourteen was the cutoff age for getting new papers, and she was fifteen. Because of her height and assured manner, she seemed even older.

"Name?" said the clerk

"Anna Morozova."

"Age?"

"Fourteen."

The clerk looked up from her paperwork. She gave Zhanna a fleeting once-over.

"Date of birth?" she said, meeting Zhanna's eyes.

"December 25, 1927."

"Okay," the clerk said. She stamped the document—a green paper—and handed it to Zhanna.

They were now officially Anna and Marina Morozova—trapped in false identities but liberated from daily fear, though not from lice-ridden beds, rotten cucumbers, and the heartache of knowing they would never see their parents and grandparents—or Kharkov—ever again.

Chapter Fourteen

With their new Anna and Marina identification papers safely in hand, Zhanna and Frina settled into life at the orphanage in the summer of 1942 and daydreamed of real liberation. Their favorite pastime was going up to the roof and looking east for the Red Army, which they expected to arrive any day.

"I see them!" Zhanna, the eternal optimist, would cry, pointing at explosive little puffs suddenly dotting the horizon. But it was always just another stray round of German artillery, never the Red Army. Much closer to the rooftop, just two hundred miles due west of Kremenchug near the town of Vinnitsa, was Hitler himself, conducting the Eastern Front strategy from his secret headquarters, code-named Werewolf.

Zhanna and Frina took turns on an old upright piano they found in the orphanage, playing folk songs and singing with the young children. German soldiers posted nearby would hear Chopin and Schubert drifting out the window and saunter over.

The piano had never been played so much or so well. The orphanage director was inspired to have it professionally tuned, and to use Zhanna to ensure that he got his money's worth.

"Tell the tuner I will not pay him until you play the piano and say it is tuned correctly," he said.

Zhanna didn't want the job. In fact, she wished the tuner was not coming at all. She and Frina grew nervous every time a stranger visited the orphanage, fearful it might be someone who recognized them from their performing days in Kharkov. She couldn't tell the director that, and she could not refuse to test the tuner's work without making the director suspicious.

"Okay," she told him, "I can do that."

The tuner was a short, hunchbacked man with an air of intelligence and formality. His name was Misha Alexandrovich. He opened his bag of tools and for the next two hours tightened bolts, tapped strings, pumped pedals, and plunked keys. Finally satisfied, he began to pack up his tools.

Zhanna, who had been watching him work from a polite distance, approached the tuner.

"Excuse me," she said sheepishly, "but the director said I must try the piano before he pays you."

He looked at Zhanna quizzically. "You can play?"

"A little."

"With both hands?"

"Yes, with both hands—and at the same time," Zhanna said archly, suppressing a grin.

"Okay then," he said, "let me hear something."

Misha took a seat and prepared to be unimpressed. What was this child going to play? "Three Blind Mice"? "Twinkle-Twinkle, Little Star"?

Zhanna sat down and raced through a C-major scale to warm up. The tuner's eyes widened. Then she played a Chopin waltz. He straightened up in his seat.

"What else can you play?"

Zhanna sped through passages of Beethoven and Bach. Misha stood up and spread his arms wide.

"This is unbelievable!" he said. "There is no one in Kremenchug who plays this well. You are coming with me. You must play for the director of the music school."

A shiver went up Zhanna's spine. The last thing she wanted was to leave the remoteness and anonymity of the orphanage for the spotlight of a music school where she and Frina would be on very public display.

"That is very flattering," she said, "but we are happy right here."

"Happy? You are starving to death here. You will be fed at the music school. You will play on a grand piano instead of this old upright. Your artistry will be appreciated. Why in the world would you not want to go?"

A person would have to be crazy not to go. There was only one reason, and it was unmentionable. The tuner shrugged his shoulders and left, but early the next morning he was back and not to be denied. They had to go, or risk being thrown in an asylum for crazy people. Reluctantly, Zhanna and Frina went with Misha to the music school in the center of town and played for the director, Professor Bulbenko, a grandmotherly figure.

She was a wonderful lady, so alive and sweet. She went wild for our playing. "You have to live here and practice! I will find a place for you!" We tried very hard to say no. But she adored music so much and was

begging us to stay. And the tuner was agreeing with
her. So there was nothing to do but move into new
quarters.

It was a dramatic upgrade in living conditions. The school
had no dormitories, so the professor put two cots in a practice
room, next to the piano. There was a big window with a lovely
view of the grounds. The toilet was in a wooden shed outside,
but the "bedroom" was lice-free. Word of the in-house prodigies
spread quickly among students and teachers at the school, bringing the girls unwanted attention, but they felt safe there. Then
one day Professor Bulbenko asked a favor that filled Zhanna
with silent panic.

"We have a theater where our students are required to perform for the Germans," the professor said. "There is only one piano accompanist for the singers and dancers, but she has a little
baby and cannot always be there. We need your help—you must
play. We have no other concert-level pianists."

I have spent months running and hiding from the
Nazis, and now you are going to put me—a fugitive
Jew—on a stage before hundreds of German soldiers?

This is what Zhanna wanted to say—to scream—to the professor. Instead, she mustered a tight smile. "Of course," Zhanna
said, "I will be happy to play."

The next day she went to meet the director of the theater.
She wore the same plain dress she wore almost every day, and
the same pair of weather-beaten shoes she had worn since leav-

ing Kharkov. Her big toe was sticking out of a hole in one shoe. A gaggle of the young dancers and actors were loitering on the lawn outside the theater when Zhanna arrived.

They were all very well-dressed, and when they saw my toe sticking out they burst into laughter. It was not funny to me. These clothes were all I had. I was ashamed and embarrassed. It hurt me so much. I thought, "I will never forget this."

Red-faced but dry-eyed, Zhanna marched past the sneering onlookers into the theater. The director was so desperate for another pianist to accompany the dancers, singers, and other entertainers that he didn't even ask Zhanna to audition.

"I would like you to start immediately," he told Zhanna.

"What do you want me to play?"

"Everything," he said.

Zhanna laughed. *"Everything?"*

"The professor says you are the finest musician in Kremenchug," he said. "You will be paid higher than anybody in the theater."

Maybe now I can buy some shoes, Zhanna thought. Frina was hired, too, but her salary was lower because she did not perform solo and had no experience as an accompanist. Her playing was limited to four-hand pieces with Zhanna, a skill Regina Horowitz had taught them at the Kharkov conservatory, never imagining it would someday be a tool of survival.

It gave Zhanna great satisfaction to know that she was making more than her taunters—the dancers and singers who now depended on her for music—but the hundreds of rubles she received were worthless since there was nothing to buy. For Zhanna, playing well was the best revenge and the director soon gave her the opportunity—a solo performance.

For the occasion, Professor Bulbenko made Zhanna a knee-length dress from white silk, using her high standing to procure the rare finery amid wartime scarcity and hardship. Zhanna's dark hair was in pigtails. And she was wearing new shoes. The concert hall was packed, mostly German soldiers with a sprinkling of Italians and Viennese. The Führer himself might well have slipped into the darkened hall. He was a music lover—music was said to be his only sure source of relaxation and diversion from the war—and Kremenchug was only a few hours by train from his command bunker at Werewolf. But in one respect his presence in the hall would have been a breathtaking act of hypocrisy.

A central justification of Operation Barbarosa—the invasion of the Soviet Union—was Hitler's stated belief that Russians were *Untermenschen*—subhumans—as was their culture. Hitler embraced Richard Wagner as the exemplar of racially pure German music and insisted that Jews had no original culture or art of their own. He banished them from concert halls in Germany. Yet his large private collection of recordings included the work of Jewish and Russian musicians such as Tchaikovsky, Borodin, and Zhanna's hero, Rachmaninoff. Was it really surprising that the murderer of so many Jews was a hypocrite in his musical tastes, in addition to everything else, as he was himself part Jewish?

Waiting backstage to make her entrance, Zhanna was nervous, but not about the music. She was playing a piece she had performed many times—the Chopin Scherzo in B-flat Minor.

It was a piece I never forgot. I could sit down and play
it in the middle of the night. In the beginning there
is suffering and indecision. Nobody knows what the
story is going to be. Immediately after the suspenseful
opening, fireworks begin. Turn the page and right
away the glorious Chopin melody starts, as though he
wrote it for a singer, so calming in a way, so romantic
and happy. It ends in fantastic victory. It's a heroic
piece—electrifying.

Watching from the wings as the hall filled, Zhanna had only one fear—that she would be recognized, that someone in the audience would shout, "She's a Jew!" But even greater than that fear was the burning anger she still felt toward the singers and dancers who had mocked her. She saw them taking seats in the back of the hall

I was still angry at being laughed at for my shoes.
When I walked out to play it was going to be for them.
I thought, "Let's see if you ever laugh at me again."

The house lights dimmed, the spotlight shone on the grand piano at the center of the stage.

"Gentlemen," the director announced, "for your pleasure this evening, performing Chopin's Scherzo in B-flat Minor— Miss Anna Morozova!"

Zhanna entered, bowed to the audience, and settled herself

at the piano. She looked down for a moment, hands in her lap. Could she summon the passion that Chopin's piece demanded— for *this* audience? Was it not a betrayal of her parents and grand-parents?

Her heart raced. Her mind reeled backward. She was on the road to Drobitsky Yar again. Her father was placing his winter coat over her shoulders. She was looking into his eyes as he spoke his final words.

"I don't care *what* you do—just live!"

Ready now, reinforced by her father's spirit, Zhanna looked up, cast a final sideways glance at the soldiers, and raised her hands to the keyboard.

The soldiers listened in amazement to the big sound coming from the slender figure on stage, Zhanna's hands rising and falling in a blur, attacking—then caressing—the keys. She spread her arms as far as she could reach, to strike the climactic notes at the far ends of the keyboard.

Suffering . . . indecision . . . fireworks . . . *victory*.

The hall erupted in thunderous applause, the soldiers on their feet whistling and shouting "Bravo! Bravo!" Zhanna exited the stage, but they kept bringing her back for encores. As she made her final bow, Zhanna looked past the soldiers to the stunned dancers and singers sitting motionless at the back of the hall.

Now let's see if you will ever laugh at me again.

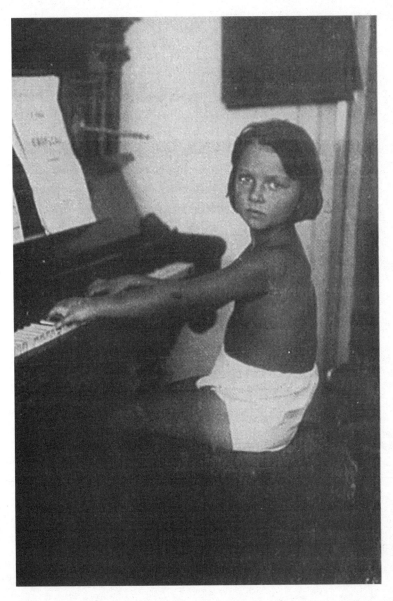

Zhanna, age 6, already at the piano at her home in Berdyansk

Zhanna's father,
Dmitri Arshansky,
in the winter coat
he gave her when
she escaped from
the march to
Drobitsky Yar

Select members of the faculty from Kharkov Conservatory.
Professor Luntz is third from the left, with glasses

The performing troupe in Kremenchug, 1942. Zhanna is in the second row from the top, in the middle, looking to the right, away from the camera. Frina refused to be photographed.

The copy of Chopin's Fantasy Impromptu Zhanna took with her when she and her family were exiled from Kharkov, which she retained throughout the duration of the war.

*Zhanna, (left) and Frina, in full costume and make up for
a wartime performance.*

*Lieutenant
Larry Dawson*

Landsberg Yiddish Center

Klavier-Koncert

bei Janna und Frina Arschanskaja

13. April 1946 Abends

Bejt Ichud

I

Overture Egmont	Beethoven
Janna und Frina Arschanskaja	
Sonata - D-Moll - opus 31	Beethoven
Frina Arschanskaja	
Sonata - F-Moll - (Appassionata) . . .	Beethoven
Janna Arschanskaja	

II

Valse - opus 34. No. 1	Chopin
Valse - E-Moll - op. Posth	Chopin
Etude - Ges-Dur - op. 10. No. 5 . . .	Chopin
Fantaisie Impromptu op. 66	Chopin
Janna Arschanskaja	
Nocturne - op. 9 No. 1	Chopin
Kleine Etude - F-Moll	Chopin
Prelude - G-Moll	Rachmaninoff
Frina Arschanskaja	
Scherzo a Cappriccio	Mendelsohnn
Prelude - C-Moll	Rachmaninoff
Janna Arschanskaja	
Hungarian II. Rhapsodie	Liszt
Janna und Frina Arschanskaja	

I M A R K   Buchdruckerei Karl Frank, Landsberg

The program for Zhanna and Frina's performances for Dachau survivors, 1946

Grace and Larry Dawson in their home in Virginia

Frina, taken in
Bloomington, circa 1958

1947 N.Y.

Zhanna and David shortly before they were married

Zhanna at the piano, circa 1961

Chapter Fifteen

The morning after the concert, Zhanna heard voices outside her window at the music school. She sat up in bed to listen closer. She heard something that sounded like pebbles striking glass. And was that a voice calling "Anna"?

Zhanna opened the shutter just wide enough to see out. She could not believe her eyes. Standing beneath the window were half a dozen soldiers holding flowers, cakes, and bottles of schnapps and vodka.

"Anna! Anna!" they shouted, catching a glimpse of Zhanna. "Bravo, Anna!"

This is a disaster, Zhanna thought, moving away from the window and her beseeching admirers. Her last shred of anonymity was gone forever. She now had an adoring public made up of her mortal enemies! At least they were supposed to be. In truth, most looked like boys, not much older than she.

They were very decent. They would stand by the window and serenade us. They just loved the music and wanted to keep it going. They were dying of boredom and didn't want to just drink. Some of them wanted to be close to us, but we never did that. The door was locked and no one was allowed in. The Italians were the worst. They were knocking on the door all the time, smiling, just dying to get inside to warm up and talk. It was so pathetic.

The Morozova sisters were the top act in town. They played four-hand pieces—the soldiers could not get enough of Schubert's military marches—and Zhanna performed a wide solo repertory, at one point playing the Grieg Concerto seven nights in a row by popular demand. The schnapps and vodka continued to pile up, and soon the girls were storing bottles inside their piano. It's a good thing they weren't drinkers, Zhanna thought, or there would be no shows.

But her job was not all cakes and schnapps. Zhanna spent many more hours out of the spotlight as accompanist to the instrumentalists and singers and dancers, even playing for the jugglers. She never got a day off, not even holidays. Zhanna worked hard for her worthless rubles, and for her and Frina's priceless sanctuary.

I got up every morning and went to work. I had to make sure to be on time for ballet rehearsal. Dancers are very demanding. They refused to rehearse without music. It was a lot of work, but I didn't know fatigue. If I did not show up, many friends would lose their livelihood.

And rivals, too. The entertainers who had mocked Zhanna

for her ragamuffin attire now found themselves dancing to her tunes, literally, which only intensified their envy as they watched her capture the hearts of the soldiers. Some of the dancers had evacuated from Kharkov to Kremenchug and brought rumors about the girls.

The ballerinas were mad that two little girls were so appreciated. They decided to go to the German bosses with the rumor that we were Jews. They were idiots to do this. Without us there was nobody to play and they would have no jobs.

The Nazi commandant in charge of organizing entertainment for the bored German troops in Kremenchug did not welcome the rumor that the only pianists at his disposal were Jews. His Russian mistress was the theater's leading comic actress in musicals. It was an agonizing dilemma: report the girls to the SS, or ignore the rumor and keep the troops entertained and his mistress singing.

"If you do not believe us," the ballerinas told him, "there is a woman from Kharkov who works at the theater. Her son was in the conservatory with the girls. You can ask her—she knows they are Jews."

The commandant reluctantly summoned the woman and her son to his office. Is it true the young pianists from Kharkov are Jews?

"I have heard what the dancers are saying," the mother said. "It is not true. I know these girls and their mother and father—they are not Jewish. The dancers are lying."

That was good enough for the relieved commandant, who could now soundly write off the "rumors" as jealousy. The show could go on!

The woman and her son put their lives on the line for us. Sometimes it's okay to lie. It's not just okay, it's heroic. But I was never at peace after that. The rumor was still out there. We could get caught at any moment.

Misha, the piano tuner, became a sort of father figure to the girls, their unofficial guardian and escort around town. One day he came to their room at the music school to deliver a special invitation.

"You have been asked to perform tonight in private for a small group," he said. "You will be dining with them beforehand. I will accompany you."

"Who is it?" Zhanna asked. "Teachers at the school?"

"That is all I can tell you," Misha said. "I will pick you up at seven o'clock. Wear your best dresses."

Drawing stares from onlookers for their silk concert dresses, the sisters followed Misha for several blocks until he stopped in front of a large, nondescript building. German guards were posted outside. A Nazi flag hung over the door.

"Misha?" Zhanna said, her voice rising in concern. "What is this?"

"Do not worry," he said. "They are just music lovers."

The visitors were led to a room at the back of the building. Standing in the doorway waiting for them was a German officer in full uniform. Zhanna was struck by how immaculate it was, how his boots shone.

"*Guten abend* (good evening)," he said, bowing slightly. "Please come in."

About a dozen officers rose to their feet as Zhanna, Frina, and Misha entered what appeared to be a private dining room. Some wore the gray-green of Wehrmacht field generals, with an iron cross at the throat and golden boughs on the collars. Others were in Waffen SS black. There was a brief, awkward interlude as the girls and the officers stood, feet apart, staring at each other in silence. How odd, Zhanna thought, to see them without pistols or rubber whips in their hands.

We sat at the same table and ate the same food. I cannot remember what it was, but I do remember there was coffee. Mama often gave us café au lait, mostly milk. The German coffee was black and bitter. I tasted it and thought it was horrible.

The officers were models of decorum, if not charm. The language barrier severely limited dinner-table banter. Germans do not seem to be a naturally gregarious people, Zhanna noted as minutes passed with only the sound of knives and forks on dishes. Finally, servants cleared the table and it was time for music. The officers stayed at the table while the girls crossed the small room to an upright piano. They played far into the night— Chopin, Schubert, Beethoven, Brahms.

These were very serious people, a wonderful audience. They kept saying, "Noch einmal!"—once more!—over and over.

Zhanna wanted to believe that these Germans were like the ones her father told her about, the ones he befriended in Poltava during World War I who were polite and spoke Yiddish and loved music and culture. But they were not. After occupying Kremenchug, the Nazis began mass executions of the city's Jews. They started by shooting the mayor, who was trying to protect them. Was the officer who pulled the trigger sitting across from Zhanna at dinner? Was he the one who cried "Noch einmal!" after she played *Fantasy Impromptu*?

When the girls finished playing, the officers stood and applauded, bowing in a courtly salute to the *wunderkinder* who for a short time had helped them forget the horrors of war—horrors they helped inflict. The sisters would be summoned for more command performances in the months ahead. With rumors about them swirling around Kremenchug, Zhanna wondered if some of the officers knew, or suspected, the truth. If so, they kept it to themselves for selfish reasons—those heavenly sonatas!—or for the greater good of the Third Reich.

Just as they harvested the hair, wedding rings, and gold fillings of Jews headed to the ovens, the Nazis may have calculated the sisters' value as entertainers and decided they were worth more to Hitler alive than dead. The lie posted at the gates of Auschwitz—"Arbeit Macht Frei (Work Brings Freedom)"—was true for Zhanna and Frina.

Just how high a value the Nazis placed on the sisters became clear in the late summer and fall of 1943 as the exhausted German army was in full retreat after a crushing defeat at Stalingrad. In August, the Red Army took back Kharkov. Then Kiev fell. As the Nazis fled, they returned to the scenes of their greatest crimes and tried to destroy the evidence. Special SS units were created to dig up and burn corpses at Babi Yar and at Drobitsky Yar.

Word of the advancing Red Army reached Kremenchug. For Zhanna and Frina, after months of fruitlessly scanning the horizon for their countrymen, liberation finally seemed to be in sight. But it was a short-lived mirage. Through his Russian-speaking mistress, the German commandant announced that Zhanna, Frina and the other entertainers were being evacuated with the army. They were needed to perform for *ost* workers—prisoners from Eastern Europe—in slave labor camps throughout Germany.

Zhanna was devastated. She had dreamed of the day she could return to Kharkov, to her beloved Katsarskaya Street. Instead, she was more a prisoner than ever before. She had become a precious commodity to the Germans, human bullion. Early one morning, Zhanna was startled by a sharp rapping at the door of their room at the music school. She had heard that urgent knocking before—the first time the Nazis came to their apartment in Kharkov. She opened the door to two young, un-smiling soldiers.

"Collect your belongings," one of them ordered. "You are being transferred to a new location."

The girls were taken to a building in a section of Kremenchug they had never visited. They were put in a room with two cots and no piano. For the first time since they had arrived in Kremenchug, they were not free to come and go.

*They had special guards to make sure that I would not
escape. I could not even go to the bathroom without
guards. Never. They would lead me there and stand
outside the door, then take me back to my room.*

If truth is the first casualty of war, logic is the second. Now
that the Nazis were slinking back to the Fatherland in defeat,
Zhanna and Frina felt in more danger than ever. Streaming
west with the Germans were Ukrainians—anti-Semites—from
Kharkov who had collaborated with the Nazis and would be eager to betray them.

*Our position was zero. The Kharkov people wanted
us dead, and the Germans would kill us if we tried to
escape.*

It was September 1943. Kremenchug had been home to the
sisters for eighteen months. It was time to go. German soldiers
were waiting for them in the street outside the music school.
The girls embraced Professor Bulbenko, their loving surrogate
mother who knew them only as Anna and Marina. As they said
their farewells, Zhanna suddenly was overcome by an inexpress-
ible sadness. For nearly two years, since the march to Drobitsky
Yar, she had not heard her real name—except the nights when
Mama or Papa appeared in her dreams and spoke to her.

The girls did not have to say goodbye to Misha—he was
leaving, too, with his wife and daughter. He had always hated
the Communists and feared reprisals by Stalin's secret police after the war. He told himself that wherever the train was going,

there would be a need for piano tuners.

The troupe of entertainers—Zhanna, Frina, a dozen dancers and actors, a balalaika player, and a juggler—boarded the westbound troop train under heavy guard. With them was the woman from Kharkov who had quelled the dancers' rumors about the girls, and her son, who served as the troupe's support staff, performing essential nonmusical tasks.

The train took them to a nameless place on the Polish border, an area of woods with few buildings or people where they stayed for days, without explanation. The troupe's best dancer, a handsome Ukrainian boy with dark hair and blue eyes, grew restive and plotted an escape.

He thought he could run away and hide in the woods. They found him and put him against a wall and beat him severely in front of us. It was so horrible that I cried and could not watch. So that's how running was. The civilian population could have hidden me, but I wasn't an idiot. I had my papers now. Once you have papers, you don't run away. You live on your papers.

After days in ominous limbo the troupe was put back on the train for the next leg of the journey to the still-secret destination. A born wanderer, Zhanna had always been fascinated by geography—the mystery of what lay beyond the horizon. With Frina in the seat beside her, Zhanna leaned back, closed her eyes, and thought of the happy hours she had spent with Papa poring over maps and planning trips to exotic places.

The locomotive churned west through darkness across an

alien landscape, away from Zhanna's homeland of blue skies and golden wheat fields, away from all that was familiar toward a place she had seen on the map but never in her armchair fantasies imagined she would ever see with her own eyes.

Next stop: Berlin.

Chapter Sixteen

B y late 1943, the Allied fist was slowly closing around
Nazi Germany's throat. Hitler's army had surrendered
at Stalingrad and in North Africa; Italy had been defeated; Mussolini was deposed, and the new Italian government
had declared war on Germany. All across the Fatherland, Allied
bombers struck cities, factories, and munitions sites with as little
mercy as the Luftwaffe had shown London.

Berlin, though, was still pristine when the train carrying
Zhanna, Frina, and their fellow Russian entertainers arrived at
Anhalter Bahnhof station the second week of November 1943.
After living in a ravaged war zone for eighteen months, Zhanna
was astonished by the capital of Hitler's Thousand-Year Reich in
all its gleaming, vulgar grandiosity.

I was amazed. The buildings had beautiful black
marble exteriors. All the windows were intact—the
glass shining. The streets were extremely clean, no trash.
Everything was orderly and well taken care of. I saw
Berlin the way Berlin was supposed to be, as it was
intended to be by the Führer for his chosen ones, so they

could breathe easy and enjoy their cherished sense of
superiority.

Zhanna and Frina stepped off the train onto a crowded platform patrolled by soldiers. The cavernous terminal's arched ceiling encompassed many sets of tracks and platforms. Zhanna tried not to be an awe-struck rube from the hinterland, but it was hard. She had never seen a station so grand, even in Moscow. The troupe was escorted out of the station by guards and taken up a broad boulevard—Wilhelmstrasse—past a series of stark, monumental buildings festooned with Nazi insignia. These were the headquarters for the major institutions of Nazi terror: SS, Propaganda Ministry, Air Ministry, Reich Security, Gestapo. Nearby was the Führerbunker—Hitler's subterranean lair.

From there it was only a few blocks to the place that would be the entertainers' home when they weren't performing at far-flung slave labor camps around Germany. Somehow, after two years of running and hiding, Zhanna and Frina had ended up living under the noses of their enemy, right in the lions' den, enjoying their relative "hospitality" no less.

> *It felt like they were next-door—that Hitler might be*
> *right there. We knew that we had better be good, better*
> *be lucky. If someone found out that we were Jews, we*
> *could be in the Gestapo station in two minutes. . .*

The troupe was housed in a four-story office building that had been converted into a dormitory setting—large rooms with bunk beds. It was near Alexanderplatz, a sprawling hub of social and business activity that was only a short distance from Wilhelmstrasse and the Nazi nerve center. Yet Zhanna and Frina felt less scrutinized and threatened in Berlin than in Kremenchug ,with its heavily patrolled streets.

It seemed the Nazis were too busy transporting Jews from Poland, Hungary, and other countries to Auschwitz and Dachau for extermination to bother checking their own backyard for stragglers. Besides, as far as German authorities knew, Zhanna and Frina were Anna and Marina Morozova, non-Jews who served a useful purpose for the war effort. They were free to come and go, to explore the streets and shops, using food coupons provided by their keepers to obtain bread, cheese, and wurst—a bit of sugar if they were lucky. They found that they were able to swap coffee to Germans for soap. Zhanna even began to develop a taste for dark German beer.

The girls' surreal respite from war lasted for exactly seven days. On the night of November 18, 1943, the British Royal Air Force began saturation bombing of Berlin. Zhanna was at Alexanderplatz when the air-raid sirens began to howl.

There were lots of people in the streets and the shops.
We ran for our lives to the nearest bunker. The bombing
never ceased after that, several times a night.

At this point, Zhanna was more worried about losing sleep than losing her life. With every air raid, the troupe was rousted out of bed and marched to a bunker in the basement.

*It was torture going up and down the stairs for air
raids while you were mostly asleep. I had no fear of the
bombs. We were under German bombs in Kharkov.
If it were me, I would not have gone down. We were
growing, we needed sleep, and we couldn't get it. We
were worn out and miserable.*

Their fatigue only deepened during the troupe's road trips to slave labor camps across Germany. Here they observed the fate of many non-Jewish Ukrainians—some likely their neighbors on Katsarskaya Street—who had been spared extermination but were still regarded as "subhumans." The camps were established to remedy a severe labor shortage in Germany after the Nazi *Blitzkrieg* stalled in late 1941 and early 1942. At the height, there were some twenty thousand camps with three million *Ostarbeiter* (eastern workers) scattered across the Third Reich, three quarters of them from Ukraine. The camps and the constant shortage of workers pointed up the lunatic, self-defeating quality to Hitler's genocidal mission. The Jews murdered by *Einsatzgruppen* and buried in countless ravines across the Ukraine could have alleviated the shortage, but Hitler refused to deviate from his conviction that the only good Jew was a dead Jew.

In late January 1942, senior Nazi officials (absent Hitler and SS chief Himmler) had met at Wannsee outside Berlin to hear the outline of a "Final Solution" to the Jewish "problem," which they already had begun to address by murdering tens of thousands of Jews across Ukraine. With Adolf Eichmann taking notes, security chief Reinhard Heydrich described a plan to transport all European Jews to German-occupied areas of the

Soviet Union where they would be worked to death. Ukrainian *Ostarbeiter*, occupying the circle of hell one level above the Jews, were to be worked just short of death. The Wannsee plan ultimately would be dropped because it presumed a Nazi conquest of the Soviet Union, and by 1943 the Wehrmacht was in full retreat. Instead of being sent east to a long, slow death as laborers, captive Jews would be shipped to extermination camps in Germany and Poland.

The same month that the *Einsatzgruppen* completed the liquidation of Kharkov Jews at Drobitsky Yar, the Nazis began deportation of non-Jews to labor camps in Germany. Citizens who only weeks before had watched in horror as the Arshanskys and other Jews were marched out of Kharkov under Nazi guard were now themselves being rounded up and put on trains to unknown destinations. By 1944, over two million Ukrainians would be forcibly transported to Germany to work on farms and in factories.

Before starting full-scale deportations, Nazi officials had tried to recruit Ukrainians by playing on their hatred of Stalin and promising a brighter future in Germany. An ad in a Kiev newspaper read: "Germany calls you! Go to Beautiful Germany! 100,000 Ukrainians are already working in free Germany. What about you?"

The ad campaign worked initially. The first train that left Kiev for Germany on January 20 was packed, many of the recruits no doubt attracted in part by the promise of "hot meals" en route. But as word trickled back from Germany about brutal living conditions in the camps, lines at the train station disappeared.

At one point, Hitler ordered that a half million Ukrainian

women be imported to lift the burden of housework from German women. One recruiting poster shows a Ukrainian woman in maid's clothing happily slicing cabbage into a pot as two beaming German children, a brother and sister, and their mother watch. "I live in a German family and feel just fine. Come to Germany to help with household chores." Only about fifteen thousand women were ever conscripted for involuntary kitchen duty in the Fatherland.

In most ways the life of a slave worker was indistinguishable from that of a Jew in a death camp. *Ostarbeiter* worked twelve hours a day, were given little food and primitive housing, and were hanged if they attempted to escape. Jews were required to wear a yellow star, *Ostarbeiter* a dark blue and white badge that read "OST" (German for east). There was one notable difference. Many *Ostarbeiter* who worked in German weapons factories died in Allied bombing raids. Jews in death camps never shared that fate, though they beseeched God to rain destruction on the gas chambers and ovens. Allied war planners studiously avoided bombing Auschwitz and other camps for fear of killing prisoners or inciting Nazi reprisals, causing great controversy and consternation.

They, did, however send warplanes to strafe the trains carrying Zhanna and Frina to the labor camps, not realizing the cars carried musicians, not munitions. Every time the planes swooped low and attacked, and it happened frequently, the train stopped and everyone scrambled under the cars until the shooting ended. An hour later they would be forced to repeat the drill.

Most trips lasted several weeks, though one time the troupe was gone from Berlin for three months. There were German escorts, but the Nazis didn't bother to put guards on the train.

They knew the Russians had nowhere to run.

We went from one slave labor camp to another. Every
morning we got up early and they took us to another
place. We hardly ever stayed two days in the same place.
Not one minute to get comfortable—never. You play,
you sleep, you go.

At every camp there was the almost putrid aroma of rutabaga soup. The emaciated laborers were as starved for diversion and laughter as they were for food. From a makeshift stage,
Zhanna looked out on a sea of faces and saw Poles, Czechs, Russians, Latvians, Estonians—but no Jews.

In Kharkov, the Germans told us they were taking Jews
to labor camps, but it was a lie. I knew they did not put
our parents in a labor camp.

The entertainers had little contact with the prisoners. They
stayed at separate facilities and left immediately after the show.
Most shows lasted about an hour. There was dancing, juggling,
and sometimes a comedy act. Zhanna and Frina performed four-
hand pieces and Zhanna played solo. But it was their honky-
tonk act with accordions, silly costumes, and makeup that always left the crowd wanting more.

Very few of them ever addressed us. They must have
thought of us as Nazi collaborators, and probably some
in the troupe were.

The ballerinas were certainly *trying* to be collaborators. Having failed to convince the Nazi authorities in Kremenchug that Anna and Marina were closet Jews, the dancers decided to try again in Berlin. They went to the German who was in charge of the troupe. And once again the mother and son from Kharkov came forward to lie for the sisters.

> *They told him we were not Jews, and that's all he needed to hear. He was very relieved. He needed us. We didn't drink, we didn't run around, and we could play.*

The Germans had tuned out the perfidious ballerinas like so many little boys who cried wolf one too many times. Far greater danger lay in chance encounters with strangers. At one of the remote labor camps, out of curiosity and sheer boredom, Zhanna and Frina agreed to go for a car ride with two men from the camp office.

They piled into the backseat of the four-door sedan. The girls had been on buses and trains, but this was their first time in a passenger car, and they were fascinated. They ran their hands across the leather seats. The driver exited the camp and went a mile or so before turning down a small road that led into thick woods. It didn't seem right to Zhanna.

"Where are we going?" she said.

The men just laughed.

"We want to go back," she said.

The men said nothing and kept driving deeper into the woods and laughing.

Frina turned to Zhanna with a panicked look. "What can

we do?" Zhanna pantomimed a silent scream, and then whispered, "Now!"

The girls started banging on the front seat with their fists and screaming like they were insane. The driver slammed on the brakes. The men said something to each other in German, rolled their eyes, and turned the car around.

We shook all over from the experience. I think we were on the verge of something very bad. We had never been raped.

Even friendly encounters at the camps could be minefields. After one labor camp performance they were approached by a prisoner, a young woman. She searched their eyes for a moment before speaking, waiting for a glint of recognition, but the sisters were silent.

"My name is Lena," she said. "I am from Kharkov. I lived in the same building with your cousin, Tamara. I have heard you play before in her apartment."

Zhanna turned pale. Her heart raced ahead of her mind, and without thinking she blurted out, "That's impossible! You have the wrong people. We have no cousin Tamara."

"No, I am sure. You are Zhannachka and Frinachka," Lena said, using nicknames known only to friends and acquaintances. "Your teacher was Professor Luntz."

At the sound of their beloved teacher's name, the girls began to weep.

"I beg you not to tell anyone," Zhanna said. "The Germans do not know we are Jews. They do not even know our real names."

"I will tell no one," Lena said, and then a guard came and led her away. The sisters never saw her again. Yes, Lena had promised to keep their secret, but she was only human, Zhanna thought. A careless remark to the wrong person at the camp could find its way back to Berlin where the authorities might decide the two Jewish impostors had outlived their usefulness and should join their ilk at Auschwitz.

That was the kind of life we were living.
We never knew.

Chapter Seventeen

For Zhanna and Frina, marking time in Berlin between harrowing train trips to labor camps, June 6, 1944, was just another day. The Nazi Propaganda Ministry a few blocks from their dormitory neglected to inform Berliners that Allied forces had landed on the beaches of Normandy that day, marking the beginning of the end for the Führer.

So for Zhanna and Frina, D-Day was just another day with not enough to do and no expectation that the next day, or week or month, would be any different. The nightly bombings by Allied planes disrupted their sleep without bringing any real hope of liberation. Zhanna frequented Alexanderplatz, rode the buses, and went to German movies with no subtitles. She was desperate for diversion.

One day she heard a rumor that a black man, an American, had been spotted at a nearby restaurant. Her interest was piqued. She had seen only one black person in her life—a performer in a circus that visited Kharkov—but her father's picture books had given her a fascination for Africans. She had never seen an American, except in silent movies she saw as a child in Berdyansk. Zhanna organized a group of friends to go check out the exciting rumor.

It was true! There was an elderly black man, with salt-and-pepper hair, sitting by himself at a table. We sat down and talked with him in broken German and had some beer. He loved the attention. It was a delightful occasion.

As nerve-racking as they were, the train trips were a welcome relief from the tedium of Berlin. One time they were taken to a camp in Czechoslovakia and it felt like a holiday to Zhanna.

Once we were in Czechoslovakia it was a different world. It was like a dreamland. The Czechs were the handsomest people I had ever seen, and also the nicest. I adored everything about the country. I did not want to leave.

Sometimes the trip organizer would split up the troupe and leave one of the sisters in Berlin. Zhanna no longer worried about leaving Frina alone. At fifteen, she bore scant resemblance to the timid little girl who had doted on her doll collection. She was as tall as Zhanna and a strong personality in her own right. Musically, she had matured as an artist. Zhanna and Frina were now equal partners in their odyssey of survival.

The pace of exterminations at Auschwitz peaked in the summer of 1944 with the arrival of 400,000 Jews from Hungary, even as the Nazis' military position continued to deteriorate. With Allied forces closing in on German soil from the east and from the west, life in Berlin grew more dangerous for foreigners, especially Russians, who would now bear the brunt of the Germans' anger and shame at their impending defeat.

*The Germans panicked and started snatching young
men off the street. We lost three or four wonderful
friends from the troupe. The SS took them and we never
heard anything about them. One of the boys was a
dancer, the most beautiful thing you have ever seen, a
prince. He was gone forever.*

Zhanna spent little time dwelling on the past and all she had
lost, or on a future that might never happen. Nothing is so un-
yieldingly in the present as war.

*The past was obliterated and the future was a space
without borders or guideposts—it was too big to think
about. My mind couldn't construct a situation with
teachers' studios and people learning. So the idea of
continuing our studies was dormant or gone and we
never talked about it.*

Zhanna had heard enough rumors about shallow graves and
ovens to guess the fate of her parents and grandparents. Imagining it was an agony she could not afford as she summoned the
will to go on. She could not allow herself to become a hostage to
her own memories. And she never did—except the day a mystery guest came to the troupe's dormitory.

All they were told was to gather in a small concert hall—
really a converted meeting room—for a special performance of
some kind. Zhanna and Frina took seats near the front. They
were excited to see a piano. But Zhanna wondered: Who plays
concerts in the middle of a war zone—unless they are prisoners?
A man entered the room, walked slowly to the center of the stage

and bowed to the audience. At first, Zhanna did not recognize this sad face. Then she gasped.

It was Victor Topilin.

The only time Zhanna had seen Victor Topilin, it was a magical moment. She was eight years old, sitting cross-legged on the stage of a packed concert hall at the Kharkov Conservatory, transported by the virtuosity of the two artists a few feet away. Topilin and violinist David Oistrakh played Mendelssohn's Concerto in E Minor that night. Zhanna felt "like heaven descended on me."

Oistrakh and Topilin brought out every bit of spirit that Mendelssohn put into the piece. It is enough to melt a stone, but this performance was a once-in-a-life event. I sensed something precious coming out of the piano which I never forgot.

Now, almost a decade later, they met again in a remote circle of hell, both captive entertainers. A German soldier discreetly blocked the only door to the room as Topilin sat down to play Bach, Beethoven, Chopin, and Schumann's Toccata, Opus 7.

He played magnificently. When he got to Schumann's Toccata, I sobbed because it was beautiful, so perfect. I was in heaven again.

Zhanna wanted to go up afterward and thank Topilin and remind him of the night in Kharkov. But she was overcome by her memories and her grief. She stood and watched as the two guards led Topilin away, out of her life once again.

I was crying too hard. All the memories—our parents,
Kharkov, Berdyansk—they all came back when I heard
the music. It was just too much for me. Too much beauty
in hell. But suddenly I understood why I must return to
school, to a great teacher and a musical life. I wanted to
play this way, like Topilin, when the war ends, but it
seemed that Hitler couldn't kill enough.

A fresh hell was fast descending on Berlin. By early spring
1945, much of the city had been destroyed by Allied bombing.
Food was in short supply. The Nazi propaganda machine was
enflaming civilian fears with horrific stories of rape and plunder
by the advancing Red Army.

Berlin was no place for human beings. The city around
me was a heap of rubble. There was constant shooting
and sounds of war. I needed to run away from the fire.
The only way to survive was to get on a train and head
south. But I felt I was betraying my countrymen.

It was a grudging decision for Zhanna. Since the day the
Nazis marched her out of Kharkov, Zhanna had dreamed of liberation and returning to Russia. She spent untold hours on the
roof of the orphanage in Kremenchug scanning the horizon in
vain for the Red Army. Finally, the Russians were coming—and
she would not be there.

Markov would. Markov was the troupe's balalaika player, its
leading Lothario, and a true believer in Communism, committed to returning home after the war. He begged Zhanna to stay
in Berlin, to marry him and go back to Russia.

I just couldn't go back with Markov. He was a terrific
soul but unbearable with women. He was after me all
the time, grabbing at me. I found myself running away
from him as fast as I could.

Zhanna was not abandoning her dream, just deferring it.
That also delayed the day she had to confront an unbridgeable
gap between herself and Frina in their feelings for their homeland. Zhanna was still attached umbilically to Mother Russia—
Frina was separated at birth and never wanted to go back. She
was totally unsentimental about Russia and her childhood—not
surprising since she had spent much of it battling illness and living in the shadow of her big sister.

Frina didn't have a chance at life in Russia. She was
afraid of it. She was the baby in the family until the
war began. I had a life from the minute I walked out of
the gate when I was three. It was all too much sorrow
for Frina. She wanted something different.

So Zhanna, Frina, and the other surviving members of the
troupe joined the chaotic mass exodus of German civilians from
besieged Berlin. The best chance for survival was to head south
to Bavaria where the Americans were said to be in control. The
sisters each carried a battered suitcase and a small accordion—
instruments of survival. As long as they could make music, they
thought, they could stay alive.

The refugees were packed together in train cars shoulder-to-
shoulder, without food, water, or bathrooms. The sullen Ger-

mans around them, humiliated and embittered by the sudden collapse of their world, were enraged by the sound of Russian being spoken.

"Verfluchte Auslander!"—curses to foreigners—they screamed at Zhanna and Frina.

The angry mob rained spit and obscenities on the terrified girls. It pressed in tighter and tighter. Zhanna felt as if her bones were being crushed.

I thought they were trying to murder us, but we were so jammed together it was impossible for them to use their arms in a harmful way. Otherwise, I think they would have choked us.

Mercifully, the mob hysteria subsided, overtaken by exhaustion. The 300-mile journey from Berlin to Augsburg in Bavaria took six days, stopping frequently to let passengers take cover from strafing by Allied planes. Zhanna stood up the whole time, barely sleeping, and speaking hardly at all, afraid of instigating another outburst.

Sometimes the train stopped and we would get out to stretch. One time I found a little house with a piece of wall that I could lean on. It was a luxury to lean where you didn't have to lean on another human being. I immediately fell asleep standing up. Sleep was like bread and air.

In Augsburg, the Russians and the German refugees went

separate ways. After a week spent mostly in the rail station, Zhanna, Frina, and the other Russians were put on another train, with no Germans this time, and taken even farther southwest to Kempten, fifty miles from the Austrian border and a world away from the looming Armageddon in Berlin.

On April 23, 1945, the Red Army entered Berlin. A week later, Hitler committed suicide in the *Führerbunker,* a short distance from Alexanderplatz. Far to the south at the other end of Germany, for the first time in what seemed like an eternity, Zhanna and Frina slept soundly.

Chapter Eighteen

A quaint, picture-postcard place at the foot of the Allgäu Alps, Kempten, Germany, was virtually unscathed by war. The only ruins were Roman. Nestled amid green valleys and snowy mountaintops, the 2,000-year-old town was a deeply tranquil place, conducive to sleep. And for a while, that was all Zhanna, Frina, and the other members of the troupe did.

> For the first time in years, we had no fear of bombing.
> We never had uninterrupted sleep in Berlin. Our bodies
> were deprived and needed replenishment. We slept
> twenty hours a day for a month. That's all we did—
> sleep and wait for the war to end. We knew Germany
> was finished, kaput.

Germany surrendered on May 7, 1945. V-E Day—Victory in Europe—triggered wild street celebrations from Moscow to Paris to New York. But for Zhanna and Frina deep in the heart of drowsy Bavaria, the war ended not with a bang but a question:

Where were the Americans?

The Allies had divided Germany into four zones of control—the British in the northwest, the French in the southwest, the Russians in the east, including Berlin, and the Americans in the south. The girls believed the American zone would be the safest. And they had found safety in Kempten. But, so far, no Americans—a big disappointment. The girls were impatient to see this exotic species up close. They thought V-E Day might finally be the day.

We were feverish to get out on the streets and meet our liberators. We thought we would be dancing and jumping with happiness until we dropped. Our elation had no limits—like our agony the day we heard Molotov on the radio announcing that Russia had been invaded by a sea of Germans.

Somewhere in the back of their minds were practical questions of what would come next—who would feed and house them, now that they were freed from Nazi bondage?—but they were lost in the euphoria of the moment. The sisters put on their concert clothes—matching knee-length silk skirts and blouses—and hit the streets. They were deserted. Light rain cast a muffling gray over the ghost town. So this is what defeat feels like, Zhanna thought. They walked for hours in the rain, up and down streets and alleys, looking for any sign of the conquering Americans.

We never saw a soul. The only thing we saw move was
a window shutter. We would see a tiny bit of space
between the shutters, someone peeking out, and then
closing it. The people were scared. We walked until we
were exhausted and never found an American.

Feeling like brides who had been left standing at the altar, the girls returned to the vacated school where they were being temporarily housed with the other entertainers. That night they toasted the end of the war with watery apple juice—surely the smallest and soberest V-E celebration on the globe.

In the ensuing days, as it became apparent no army was coming to rape and pillage, the German townspeople began cautiously to emerge from homes. The air was thick with rumors about the Americans. GIs dancing with local girls at a beer hall? That was believable. But Zhanna and Frina scoffed at the rumor that an American officer had been seen in an office with his boots propped on a table.

That was inconceivable to us. You eat or do work on a
table—you don't put your feet up! Nobody in the world
would do that. It's disrespectful. We decided we had to
see that!

As the girls searched for the American with elevated feet—or *any* American, since they still had not met one—they encountered something even more comical and bizarre: the English language.

One day I was directed to an office for some question about a document. I was told there would be Americans but they turned out to be English—two women and a man in military outfits. It was the first time I heard English. I thought, "They must be kidding—this cannot be a language!" It was so awful that I thought they were putting on a show to amuse me.

Finally, a week after V-E Day, Zhanna met her liberators. She had been sent to an office in Kempten to pick up paperwork for the sisters' transfer to a displaced persons camp. Entering the office, Zhanna was stopped cold by what she saw in front of her. Sitting behind the desk was an American soldier—with his feet on the desk!

The incredible rumor was true. Zhanna stared at the American—with his big smile and funny uniform and unpolished boots casually tilted against the desk—as if he were a unicorn in her garden.

"Can I help you, young lady?"

Zhanna didn't understand. All she knew to do was say her name. But which one? Since the moment she learned the war ended, Zhanna had thought of only two things: Returning to Russia, and getting her name back. "Anna Morozova" belonged to the Nazis. She could not get her mother and father and grandparents back, or her old life in Kharkov, but she could get her name. She could tell the smiling American, "My name is Zhanna Arshanskaya!" But Anna Morozova had been her protective shield for more than three years. It was on her green I.D. card. She was not yet ready to cast it aside, to trust again. She looked the American in the eye.

"Anna Morozova," she said, pointing to herself.

Zhanna was in greater danger than she knew, or could have imagined. It was rooted in her dream of returning to Russia, where she expected to be greeted with open arms.

I expected a celebration. I just knew that Russians couldn't wait to have us back to help rebuild the country. And I thought that returning Jews would be in special favor because Hitler had tried to exterminate all of us. Nothing else made sense to me—nothing else seemed logical.

Like father, like daughter. Just as "logic" and his worship of German music had blinded Dmitri to signs of the coming Holocaust, Zhanna's reverence for her homeland would not let her hear the whispers that refugees returning to Russia faced almost certain death or exile to a Siberian labor camp. Stalin considered surrender a criminal act, even if a soldier was wounded, had lost his weapon or had run out of ammunition. "In Hitler's camps there are no Russian prisoners of war, only Russian traitors, and we shall do away with them when the war is over," he told a foreign reporter. It was not an empty threat—Stalin was describing the exact fate of Red Army prisoners from the 1939-40 Winter War in Finland. One of the most notorious cases of Stalin's mercilessness concerned Lieutenant General Mikhail Lukin, commander of the Soviet Nineteenth Army, who was seriously wounded and taken prisoner. He returned home without legs—amputated by Nazi doctors—but with his loyalty intact after refusing entreaties to join a group of Russian collaborators and calling their leader a traitor to his face. Lukin's stoicism was rewarded with the same brutal interrogation visited on other returnees and a prison term.

Stalin played no sentimental favorites in his contempt for surrender. Stalin's oldest son, Jacob, a major in the Red Army, was wounded and taken prisoner in early fighting on the Eastern Front. When a reporter asked about him, Stalin said, "I have no son called Jacob." When his father's words reached him via a radio broadcast in the POW camp, the devastated Jacob committed suicide by throwing himself on electrified barbed wire.

Stalin was equally unforgiving toward civilians. Those who "allowed" themselves to be taken prisoner by the invading Nazis were traitors. True patriots would have fled east to the Urals or beyond, Stalin declared. And those who remained, like the Arshanskys, were expected to commit suicide rather than fall into Nazi hands.

Zhanna did not know about the meeting at Yalta, in her own backyard in Ukraine, that would make a mockery of her homecoming dreams. Buried in the agreement signed by Roosevelt, Churchill, and Stalin in February 1945 was a provision requiring return of prisoners of war and displaced persons to their home countries, whether they wanted to go or not—forced repatriation.

"All Soviet citizens liberated by forces operating under United States command will, without delay after their liberation, be separated from enemy prisoners of war and will be maintained separately from them in concentration camps until they have been handed over to the Soviet authorities," the provision read.

Allied leaders saw no reason to read between the lines of the straightforward language, nor did tens of thousands of Soviet exiles who streamed to reception centers in May 1945 after the parties had worked out logistical details of repatriation. From June 10 to 13, in a small miracle of bureaucratic efficiency, 101,000 Soviet citizens *a day* began the journey home. By September, more than two million Soviet nationals had been repatriated—voluntarily—from Germany, Austria, and Czechoslovakia. But approximately 5.5 million Soviets, military and civilian, were left in enemy territory at the end of the war, so the initial influx was far short of the total repatriation Stalin pursued with an urgency and vengeance that the Allies at first did not apprehend.

Essentially, Stalin saw the 5.5 million as escaped prisoners whose crime was being outside the borders of the Soviet Union when the war ended. They were presumed guilty of treason until proven innocent—and must be brought back, by force if necessary, lest they spread "lies" about Stalin's rule or form an exile movement that could threaten him. It was an expression of the same paranoia that fueled Stalin's attempt to wipe out the small population of kulaks, or wealthy peasants, whom he perceived as likely leaders of a peasant revolt. Stalin's drive for total repatriation had a simple twofold purpose, expressed by an officer for the counter-intelligence agency SMERSH, an acronym for words that mean "death to spies."

"In the first place, they were undesirable witnesses against Communism and the Soviet system," he said of the un-repatriated. "Secondly, the Soviet Union had suffered colossal human losses in the war and was short of manpower."

The postwar need for able bodies to rebuild the Soviet economy probably prevented Stalin from killing as many of the returnees as he would have liked. It also explains why the repatriation agents he sent to displaced persons camps in German and other western zones did not simply shoot Soviets on sight. Those who were not killed upon their return home were hardly granted clemency, however. Most were sent to *gulags* or condemned to a lifetime of hard and dangerous labor.

In late 1945, as the terrible fate awaiting returnees became more widely known and Stalin's repatriation agents became more aggressive in their "recruitment" efforts, Soviets in the DP camps grew hysterical with fear. There were widespread reports of suicide. In January 1946, eleven Soviets at a DP camp at Dachau committed suicide, nine by hanging themselves from a noose attached to a bunk bed. At a camp in Leipzig, a desperate old man with an ax in his hand confronted a Soviet agent: "Here is my ax, and here is my head. Chop it off, but I won't go back."

Under the prevailing Yalta agreement, reluctant American soldiers were obliged to assist the Soviet agents in their nefarious mission. A DP worker described one such nightmare scenario. "I saw a woman throw her baby out of a building to her husband. He tried to run, but U.S. soldiers caught him and his baby."

Ultimately, five million Soviets would return home from Eastern Europe and western occupation zones, leaving behind about 500,000 "nonreturners," among them Zhanna and Frina. They were unaware of the betrayal at Yalta and the unfolding tragedy the day they said goodbye to Kempten and boarded the train for a displaced persons camp near Munich—the last stop before being delivered into the hands of Stalin's inquisitors. Their pity, if they possessed any at all, was not likely to be roused by two girls who had spent the war entertaining Nazi officers at dinner while Russian soldiers lay dying in the snow.

Chapter Nineteen

On V-E Day, Zhanna and Frina were among eight million refugees, slave workers, prisoners of war, and Nazi death camp survivors stranded in Germany and Austria, "liberated" but homeless. The Allied powers chartered the United Nations Relief and Rehabilitation Administration—UNRRA—to run hundreds of camps where the displaced persons could live while waiting to return to their homelands, or perhaps emigrate to another country.

Like many DP camps, Funk Kaserne near Munich was an abandoned army barracks and bore disconcerting reminders of its recent past, such as a Nazi Reich Eagle on the front gate. Otherwise, it provided clean if spartan accommodations for the five thousand temporary residents.

Zhanna and Frina were anomalies. Except for death camp survivors, there were few Jews in the DP camps—or anywhere in Europe. The Nazis had seen to that. Most Russian refugees were Ukrainian and ended up in camps in the Soviet sector in northern Germany. At Funk Kaserne, Zhanna, Frina, and the other members of the troupe were lost in a sea of Italians and French.

The Italians were a lot of fun, especially to an eighteen-year-old girl like me. They were masters of smiles and running after women. The French women were very snappy in fixing themselves up. I don't know where they got it, but they always smelled of perfume. However, their standards were not up to ours in keeping the facilities clean. They didn't care how sloppy it was.

Sadly, neither the French nor the Italians were able to lend the culinary prowess of their homeland to the dismal menu at Funk Kaserne. The daily fare consisted of thin rutabaga soup, bread, hard cheese, and occasionally the American *piece de resistance*—Spam. The only thing at Funk Kaserne worse than the food was the boredom. Now that the Nazis were defeated, tedium was Zhanna's greatest enemy.

Or so it seemed on the surface. What could be safer than a United Nations-run camp in the American-occupied zone? Once again, the devil was in the details of the Yalta agreement, which permitted Soviet agents to circulate in the camp. Latvians and Lithuanians began to disappear from their barracks at night, and it was discovered that rogue agents were abducting the refugees and holding them in a basement for transport to the Soviet Union. When the American head of the camp learned of the kidnappings, he raided the basement, freed the hostages, and kicked the Soviets out of Funk Kaserne—Yalta be damned. He became the instant folk hero of the camp.

Somehow, though, the story did not give Zhanna second thoughts about returning to Russia. Hers was not a conscious decision; it was a compulsion as blind as the migratory instinct of a bird, so powerful it overrode all reason.

I did not connect myself to what was happening in the camp. I thought I had a privileged position. I would go home and tell everyone how we were treated by the Germans, and how we lived every moment for their defeat. It would be impossible for the Russians not to understand.

Zhanna proceeded to make arrangements with Russian army officers—not the renegade security agents—for her departure from Funk Kaserne. No other members of the troupe were going. Yet, Zhanna was confident Frina would follow her.

I couldn't think any other way. We must remain together. We are a family this way.

On a warm night in late June, the troupe gathered in the barracks to say goodbye to Zhanna and Frina as the Russian officers looked on. Zhanna had a last-minute concern.

"Will I be allowed to take my accordion?"

"Da! Da!" said an officer in delighted tones. "It's time to go. The car is waiting."

As Zhanna gathered up her things and friends crowded around for final hugs, a voice pierced the commotion.

"I am not going."

The room fell silent. Zhanna turned and stared at Frina. She was standing in the middle of the room with her arms folded across her chest. Zhanna was confused.

"You are not going?"

"I am not going," Frina said.

"This cannot be!" Zhanna said.

The Russian officers were growing impatient. The car outside was running. The moment Zhanna had dreamed of for so long finally had arrived, and she saw it slipping away. She walked closer to Frina and searched her sister's eyes.

I thought Frina would give in, but she didn't move. It was plain that she meant it. The decision was made for me. Leaving Frina was not a possibility.

The disgusted Russian officers stormed out of the barracks. The other members of the troupe discreetly filtered out. Zhanna slumped onto a bed. "I will never see Russia again," she thought, and began to softly weep. Frina sat in silence on the other side of the room.

Time would validate Frina's decision, born of instinct—she had no knowledge of Stalin's postwar persecutions—and reinforced by memories of a difficult childhood which repelled her as powerfully as Zhanna's halcyon memories called her home. By December 1945, the murder and exile of returning Russians by Stalin's regime had become so horrendous that General Eisenhower ordered American soldiers to cease assisting in forced repatriations.

Frina saved me from disaster in Russia. I thought it would be a celebration, but my devotion turned out to be one-sided. They wanted us to return to take our lives away. Why couldn't I see what Frina knew? She saved our lives.

Zhanna was not fatalistic, but sometimes in life, as in music, it was possible to find mystical symmetry. She had refused to let Frina go to sleep and die in a snowy field in Ukraine. And now Frina had stopped Zhanna from sleepwalking to her death. Their partnership of survival had come full circle.

"Stalin did not give a damn about us."

Zhanna's umbilical cord to Mother Russia was severed at last.

Chapter Twenty

After going through hell in Ukraine and purgatory in Berlin, Zhanna found herself in limbo at Funk Kaserne, going stir-crazy. An army base—designed for regimentation with as few amenities and distractions as possible—was a prison without walls for someone like Zhanna who was "born busy." She was free to leave the camp during the day, but there was nowhere to go and no way to get there.

*We were doing absolutely nothing, just running around
waiting for our next bowl of soup. I couldn't stand it,
so naturally I started walking. I walked and walked
around this huge camp until I came to a little building.
It was empty, so I went inside for a look.*

It was a musty-smelling hall with churchlike pews and bad lighting, but at the far end on a little stage—Zhanna couldn't believe her eyes—was a piano! It was not much of a piano, just an old upright, but Zhanna could not have been more overjoyed if she'd been Howard Carter stumbling into Tutankhamen's tomb.

*I sat down and tried it. It was an awful instrument,
just horrible, but it played. I ran back to the barracks
and announced, "There is a piano!" That's all it took.
Everyone was so bored that we decided we must put
on a show. But first we needed a permit. I marched
to the UNRRA office and asked if we could use the
empty building to put on a show. It was a quick and
unanimous yes!*

About half the troupe remained from the fifteen entertainers evacuated from Kremenchug at gunpoint by the Germans two years before. Several male dancers had been snatched off the streets by Gestapo in Berlin and were never seen again. Markov, the balalaika player and Zhanna's unrequited suitor, had stayed in Berlin to be liberated by the Red Army, and was probably dead by now. The jealous ballerinas who had tried to betray Zhanna and Frina to the Nazis had disappeared somewhere between Berlin and Bavaria.

That still left plenty of bodies to put on a show—dancers, actors and a juggler, in addition to Zhanna and Frina on piano and accordion. Word spread quickly among the camp residents starved for entertainment, and by showtime a standing-room-only crowd packed the little hall. The troupe made do with a bare stage, the creaky piano, and little else. It likely was the first time in entertainment history that juggling and Chopin's *Fantasy Impromptu* were on the same bill.

After Zhanna performed *Fantasy Impromptu*, she and Frina played four-hands, and then hoisted their accordions for a round of Russian folk songs. The hall rocked with laughter and applause from their fellow refugees, grateful for some merriment after years of misery.

Standing at the back of the hall, marveling at the sisters' performance, was the man who would change their lives forever. The entertainers were greeting fans after the show when Zhanna noticed an American in uniform striding up to the stage.

I thought, "No wonder—we have these gorgeous
Russian singers and dancers. He is coming to see them."
Nothing doing! He was heading straight for Frina and
me.

The rangy American walked up to the sisters and, seemingly oblivious to the gaggle of admirers around them, started babbling excitedly in broken German. And Zhanna thought *her* German was bad!

It was the funniest German you ever heard—a
ridiculous accent. He was so excited. He wanted to
know who we were and what else we could play. He
was out of his mind with curiosity about us. I thought
he was one funny duck. I kept asking myself, "Does he
put his feet on the table, too?"

In his crisp, button-down uniform, he had the lean, rugged good looks of Gary Cooper, but the very opposite of the actor's stern, laconic demeanor. This American waved his arms, smiled, and would not stop talking. The girls were amused. Charm is an international language.

It was so hard to understand him, but finally it came
out that he was inviting us to come to UNRRA
headquarters in Munich the next day to eat dinner
with the officers and then to play for them. Who could
say no to that? It had to be better than more rutabaga
soup.

Delighted, the American shook the girls' hands and said he would pick them up the next day at five o'clock.

"Do you realize who that is?" one of the dancers asked after he left the hall.

"I don't know—General Eisenhower?" Zhanna joked.

"He is the head of the camp."

"What?" Zhanna said, laughing. "You are telling me this funny man is the same one who freed people from the basement and kicked the Soviets out of the camp?"

"Yes, it is the same man. His name is Larry Dawson."

The girls were baffled. They went back to their barracks and spent the next twenty-four hours analyzing this peculiar American and his frenzied interest in them and their music. The next day, Larry arrived at five o'clock and took them by car to UN-RRA headquarters, a pleasant if modest house in Munich. The girls were seated at a long dining table between UNRRA officers, men and women from several European nations. The conversation was multilingual but the menu was strictly American, featuring the inevitable Spam and two items new to the girls.

White bread—oh mercy! We had never seen anything so
white. We thought it was the best thing in the world.

They were also given a dollop of something brown that Zhanna thought was mustard—until she tasted it. She couldn't decide if she liked it. It was the first food that ever stuck to the roof of her mouth. They called it "peanut butter." But how could any butter, which came from cream, be brown? Zhanna could not understand.

Nobody could explain to us what it was. I couldn't make up my mind. I thought it was crazy food.

For the girls' excited host, dinner was a distracting prelude to the real purpose of the evening. Even before the dishes were cleared he looked at Zhanna and Frina and pointed to an upright piano across the room

He wasn't fooling around. He took a chair and sat down right next to the piano as though he was going to instruct us. The moment we finished a piece, he asked to hear it again. He wanted me to play Fantasy Impromptu *over and over. "Noch einmal!" (again), he would say, just like the German officers, but in his funny American accent.*

The evening went from sublime to ridiculous when some-one sat down at the piano and began playing ballroom dancing tunes, and Larry asked Zhanna to dance.

It was very crowded and he immediately started stepping all over my feet. He had the biggest feet and

they were all over mine. It was terrible. So it was back
to the piano for me for the rest of the evening.

By the time Larry delivered the girls back to Funk Kaserne that night, to the curious stares of their bunkmates, he was already planning out their futures in his mind. They were startled when he showed up at their barracks the next morning in an agitated state.

"You know," he said, "the war is over and you have all this time on your hands. You've got to start studying and practicing again!"

"Practice?" Zhanna said. "How? We don't even have a teacher or a decent piano."

"Don't worry—I will find a piano and a place for you to practice," Larry said. "And I will teach you."

He was going to teach *them*? They were too flabbergasted to laugh, or object. Larry found a small, cottage-like building on the grounds with enough room for two cots and a piano. He procured a decent piano and sent subordinates to Munich in search of sheet music. The girls thought it was no accident that their "private" barracks and practice hall was only a short distance from Larry's office.

He was constantly stopping in to make sure practice
was going the right way, to see what page we were on,
demanding things he remembered from the records he
had heard hundreds of times when he was growing up.
Very often, other UNRRA members from the dinner
would come with Larry to see how far we had gotten
with the Beethoven sonatas he had assigned us.

Zhanna and Frina could see that Larry was just a dilettante. He had no more business instructing them than the juggler did. Yet they humored him. He was head of the camp, after all. But it was more than that. It was his awkward charm, his headlong American enthusiasm, and a transcendent passion for music which Zhanna had seen in only one other man in her life—a man no longer in her life—her father.

Larry's teaching was just outlandish. He had absolutely no idea how to get around the piano. But he was so intent and insistent—and the music was part of him. When he wasn't joking and laughing, Larry looked very serious like he was floating in some unknown space and you didn't dare to open your mouth and interrupt his search. His head was in the sky. He was walking on cloud nine.

Chapter Twenty-One

L arry Dawson was born in 1910 in Berkeley, California, the fourth of five children of Marine Col. William C. Dawson and his wife Laura. The children—four boys and a girl—were born in five different cities in the United States and Japan, reflecting the itinerant military life. The youngest, David, was born three years after Larry in New Rochelle, New York.

It was a family of hard-headed believers and impossible dreamers. Col. Dawson pulled his family out of the Catholic church in Charlottesville, Virginia, when it flew the American flag in World War I, in the belief the practice violated the separation of church and state, and put the imprimatur of religion on killing.

The Dawsons lacked the practical gene. They were living in Charlottesville when the colonel died after a long, horrible bout with rheumatoid arthritis. The family fell on very hard times. But by then, luckily, the children were old enough (Larry was thirteen) to make money doing odd jobs around town—shoveling snow, mowing grass, delivering newspapers. But then, thinking it would be cheaper to live in the country, Laura moved the family to a little house in the Blue Ridge Mountains outside Charlottesville, far from everything and the life they knew.

Laura, who had grown up wealthy with servants, attended finishing school, and depended on the colonel's income, was ill-equipped for her new hardscrabble life, as were her children. The colonel had not passed on a lot of practical know-how to his brood. His major legacy was a love of music. The family's main form of recreation was gathering round to listen to recordings of the great composers and performers. They became Larry's gold standard for life—sacred, immutable templates for judging all other performances. The rest of Larry's music education consisted of watching the keys go up and down on the family's player piano. He learned to "play" a few pieces such as the first movement of Beethoven's "Moonlight" Sonata, his fingers anticipating the robotic movement of the keys in a pianistic pantomime.

The only child to master an instrument was David, the baby of the family born in 1913, but he had talent enough for all five siblings. David began violin lessons at age six, and it was soon apparent that the music gods had been extravagant, endowing him with perfect pitch and tone, an intuitive grasp of composition, and long, slender fingers and a supple bow arm made for conjuring beauty from a wooden box and steel strings as magically as a snake charmer coaxes a cobra from its woven lair. During a visit to the University of Virginia in 1925, two distinguished musicians from New York heard twelve-year-old David play in a class setting. Their impression was reported in a story in the *Charlottesville Daily Progress*, two days before David's hometown concert debut on Nov. 15, 1926.

"That young Dawson has actually caught a spark of the rare fire of genius, seems probable. That he is endowed with an extraordinary musical precosity is already evident. Able and cautious critics who have heard him play enthusiastically assert that he is destined for the heights of artistic achievement. When Felix Salmond, eminent violoncellist, and Harold Bauer, pianist came to Charlottesville last winter, they heard Master Dawson play. In musical circles such as that to which these artists belong, flattery is not practiced, candor is the rule. Both praised his playing extravagantly, declaring it to be prodigious. Both even dared to prophesy for him."

The review of David's performance in the *Daily Progress* took up where the preview left off under a headline reading, "David Dawson, 13-year-old Violinist, Thrills Audience In Debut Concert at University." His program: Nardini's D Major Sonata, Sarasate's arrangement of Chopin's E Flat Nocturne, Massenet's "Meditation," a Mazurka by Wieniawski, and the Mendelssohn Concerto in E Minor.

"Delighting, astonishing, and at times even thrilling all who heard him, David Dawson, Charlottesville thirteen-year-old violinist, made his first formal appearance in his home city yesterday evening in Cabell Hall before an audience which showed the enthusiasm that the excellence of his recital deserved.

"Conscious of the risk of being called extravagant, we do not hesitate to pronounce his tone marvelous, both in its extraordinary strength and its surpassing beauty of quality. There is about his playing already, an amazing amount of real finish, but there is every indication in it of future mastery of technique.

"We have heard others of David's age play many of the

numbers which he presented so admirably, with a high degree of technical facility, equal or almost equal to his own. But never before have we encountered in one of his years, and but rarely in his seniors, the genuineness of musical understanding and the depth of feeling which his playing reveals.

"David Dawson has studied the violin, in all, only six years. He is now the pupil of Prof. Winston Wilkinson of the Department of Music at the University of Virginia. If ever a teacher had just cause to be abundantly proud of his pupil, it is Prof. Wilkinson. If ever a city had cause to be proud of, and to encourage to the utmost, a talented son, that city if Charlottesville."

David left home at fourteen for a scholarship at the Juilliard School of Music. Larry's pride in his little brother was so great it exceeded, though just barely, his heartbreak at saying good-bye. In ensuing years, David switched from violin to viola, and in 1939, at twenty-six he was named principal violist of the Minneapolis Symphony Orchestra under Dimitri Mitroupolos at a salary of $115 a week—enough to send money home to Virginia where the rest of the Dawsons were struggling in the aftermath of the Depression. Larry was drifting. Two years in military school when he was younger had done little to alter his recalcitrant nature. He tried college and quit after two indifferent years. He made money doing odd jobs, and the *Daily Progress* paid him for occasional freelance articles. He shared an apartment with his mother, who had moved back to Charlottesville after the other kids left home to start lives.

Larry was thirty and still searching when he met Grace Jarman at a dance. A dark-haired beauty with a no-nonsense attitude and a penetrating gaze, Grace was everything Larry was not: skilled, practical, focused. A farm girl, she knew how to butcher a hog, plant a garden, and change a tractor tire. She was on her way to finishing nursing school. The only music she had ever heard was The Grand Old Opry on radio.

Larry and Grace were married in 1941 and they scraped together $6,500 to buy a farm with 108 acres and an old house badly in need of renovation in Crozet, a village deep in the country outside Charlottesville. In his excitement, Larry sounded very much like his mother had when she moved the family to a house in the mountains.

"It didn't have central heating or electricity or a bathroom or anything," Grace said. "But Larry felt that we could move to this farm and our living expenses wouldn't be that great."

The grand plan overlooked an important detail: Larry knew nothing about farming, and had none of the aptitude required to learn.

"We had the land, and he thought that was all that was needed to be a farmer," Grace said. "Larry didn't know how much work it was just to put in a garden. You've got to till the soil and plant the seed. You've got to hoe it and keep the weeds out and all those things. He didn't know how that was. Larry had done some bush-hogging once where he got on a tractor and drove around and around and around. He didn't maintain the tractor or anything. He thought, 'I can be a farmer just' cause I *want* to be a farmer, and I'm going to do it.'"

But first Larry wanted to be a soldier. He *had* to be a soldier. He entered officer training school and ultimately was sent to West Palm Beach, Florida, where he expected to be shipped out to Europe. Grace took a two-week leave from nursing school to spend time with him before the ship sailed. At the last moment his orders changed and 2nd Lieutenant Dawson was assigned to the quartermaster corps, responsible for food, clothing and equipment for troops that did the fighting. He was inconsolably disappointed.

"He wanted to go fight," Grace said. "He thought it would be more glamorous and fun. I thought, 'You crazy nut—you can live in West Palm Beach and not be in danger and have a good salary, and you want to go off and put up with the hardships over there?' But he was idealistic like that."

Grace quit nursing school and stayed with Larry in Florida. Their first child, "Lad"—named for his dad, Laurence A. Dawson—was born there, and Grace was five months pregnant with a second son, George, when the war ended. She was ready to return to Crozet to raise a family and work the farm. But Larry was still racked by an unfulfilled yearning. Mustering helmets and C-rations had fallen well short of the contribution he had envisioned making to the war against Hitler.

When he learned the Army was looking for volunteers to assist in repatriation of war refugees in Europe, Larry knew he had to go. This was his chance to do something important for democracy and mankind. He would be in charge at one of the many camps for displaced persons in Germany. His assignment was Funk Kaserne, the abandoned German army base near Munich. His salary as an Assembly Center Director for UNRRA would be $5,500 a year plus expenses.

Grace had mixed feelings. She was losing Larry just when she needed him most, with young children and a farm to tend to. He was expected to be gone for a year. On the other hand, the war was over, so he would be safe—and, finally, fulfilled.

"I felt this was a blessing because he's always going to feel like he was passed over because he didn't get to fight, and here is a chance for him to do good work for a lot of people. He's never going to take the easy road, you know. He's going to help anybody he can, no matter what it costs himself. I was glad he finally had his dream come true."

And Grace was secretly thankful for another reason: it put off the day when she would have to watch her impossible dreamer wrestle with a plow.

Chapter Twenty-Two

At least ten times a day, Larry would leave his office at Funk Kaserne and walk a short distance to the little building he had converted into living quarters and practice hall for Zhanna and Frina. He was concerned that without his supervision they would not reach their full potential as artists. The fact that he could barely read music did not faze him one bit. Larry *knew* from recordings what the music was supposed to sound like. His challenge—his higher calling—was to take the girls' raw talent and marry it with the spirit of the music.

Never mind the notes. Larry's imagination was fixed on the picture of these young, wandering pianists who would learn under his tutelage. It was our fingers and tone and memory of the music, but he, Larry, was going to dictate how to shape it for a performance.

While Larry endlessly probed and tinkered with the sisters' keyboard technique, he had no questions about their stock life story which seemed straightforward enough. To him, they were Anna and Marina, and it stung the girls' hearts every time he uttered the names. The girls hungered to reclaim Zhanna and Frina, and decided this was a person they could finally trust. But how to raise the issue with Larry? He conveniently solved that dilemma during one of his frequent drop-ins to the practice room. His feet were propped against a table and he wore the faraway, searching expression which had become so familiar to the girls.

"If you could have anything you desired at this moment," Larry asked, "what would it be?"

The girls traded knowing looks, then Zhanna spoke.

"Our names—we want our true names back."

The faraway look gave way to perplexity. Larry put his feet on the floor and sat forward in his chair. "But I saw your papers—they say Anna and Marina Morozova."

"They are false names," Zhanna said. "We needed them to get new papers."

"Why did you need new papers with false names?"

Zhanna hesitated for a moment. "We are Jews."

Larry stared at the girls, speechless.

"We are Zhanna and Frina Arshansky. Our father was not in the Red Army—he was a candy maker and amateur violinist in Kharkov. The Germans were taking the Jews from our town to be killed and we escaped. We changed our names to survive. The rest of our family is dead."

"You should have told me earlier," Larry said.

"We were afraid—it has been so long. . . . " Zhanna said, and she began to sob.

Larry crossed the room and knelt down in front of the girls.

"Zhanna . . . Frina . . . listen to me. I will *never* let anyone hurt you. Do you understand? You are part of my family now."

*Getting our names back, telling Larry the truth—I'll
tell you what it was like. It was like the feeling on the
day the war ended when we got dressed to go look for
the Americans. A feeling that big—to be the person you
really are.*

Now, for them, the war was truly over.

It did not take long for the big thinker, the impresario in Larry, to brainstorm a coming-out party for the sisters, now that he knew their true identity. It would be their first concert since the war as Zhanna and Frina Arshanskaya. And what better audience than fellow survivors of Hitler's genocide? The girls would play for Polish Jews liberated from a place with a short, cruel name they had never heard—Dachau. It would be a concert honoring all who had "survived."

*Larry was very proud to announce that these two
Jewish girls were going to play for the freed Jews. It
would be a great celebration—the rejoicing of people
who lived through Hell together.*

It was an occasion that married Larry's love of music with the historical moment, and he was taking no chances with the music. To prepare for the concert, he told the girls, they would spend two months in Oberstdorf, south of Funk Kaserne in the Bavarian Alps, where UNRRA was housed in a palatial private home. There, in splendid and picturesque isolation, they would learn the dauntingly ambitious program he had chosen for their debut. Larry was like the man who visits the buffet table and comes back with one of everything: Beethoven, Chopin, Rachmaninoff, Mendelssohn, and Liszt—thirteen pieces in all. It was less a concert than a marathon, with Larry less a teacher than a coach pushing his runners beyond exhaustion.

Larry didn't want us to play old repertory. His principle was that we should always be learning something new. He didn't want me to play Beethoven's "Pathetique Sonata", which I knew well. I had to learn the "Appassionata" because he always loved it. Frina had to learn the D-Minor Sonata, Opus 31. I also had to learn a devilishly difficult scherzo by Mendelssohn. Horowitz was famous for it, and Larry grew up listening to his recording. So I was expected to match Horowitz.

Camp Larry did have its compensations. The wintertime Alpine scenery was breathtaking, and the girls took breaks from practicing to play in the snow, even donning skis for a few comical turns down the slopes. It was a level of luxury to which Zhanna and Frina were not accustomed.

There was a gorgeous dining room with a very long table where we had our breakfast and dinner served to us every day. The people at the table were the cream of the crop—intellectuals, aristocrats, people from the army and the government. Every day was kind of a party, and there was no fear—that was the main thing. It was tremendous not to fear.

Zhanna's only anxiety was over the program she was trying to learn, especially the "Appassionata." After all, she had spent the last four years without any formal training.

I was guessing how to knit together and bind all the parts of this massive piece, and I needed help from an experienced pianist and teacher who had touched all the keys of the composition. All I got from my coach was a lot of inspiration and unrealistic ideas.

The concert was on the evening of April 13, 1946, at the Landsberg Yiddish Center west of Munich. Larry had arranged for a temporary stage to be built in the main hall. Programs were printed in German for the "Klavier-Konzert" featuring "Janna und Frina Arschanskaja." In a different time and place, the program would have been performed in a grand concert hall for an elegantly attired audience. Into this most spartan of venues filed 1,200 Jews, gaunt and ragged from their time in the death camps. Before them on the stage stood two Ukrainian Jewish girls in pigtails and simple dresses.

The average length of a piano recital is about seventy minutes. Larry's extravaganza was almost twice that long. The thirteen-piece program began with Beethoven's *Egmont* Overture, reached a midway point with *Fantasy Impromptu*, and concluded with the sisters' four-hand arrangement of Liszt's *Hungarian Rhapsody*.

The music washed over the grateful listeners like a soft restorative rain falling on desert flowers. As the audience showered the girls with applause and bravos, Zhanna bowed and decided it was, technically, the worst she had ever played.

It was clear to me that it was probably the most inaccurate performance of my life. But realizing the concert was a celebration helped me to keep going as I was playing, wholly tied to the listeners' hearts. I was there with them, alive, with my sister, their ears connected with mine, able to hear Beethoven speak. The horror created by Hitler was defeated. I couldn't have cared less, just this one time, if the performance wasn't to my standard because it had done what we wanted—to help lift humanity to goodness again, to fill the survivors of torture with signs of life and peace without fear.

Overnight, Zhanna and Frina went from ordinary DPs to VIPs. Anna and Marina Morozova were officially dead. The sisters savored the sweet sound of their own names coming from the lips of their friends. For Zhanna, though, the spotlight of celebrity also brought a disturbing proposal, from the most unlikely source—her liberators.

The day after the concert she was summoned to a U.S. military office at the camp which she had never visited. She was seated at a table opposite a pleasant young man in uniform. She felt certain he was Jewish.

"You are a friend of our country," he said. "We need information and you might be able to help us obtain it."

"What do you mean?" Zhanna said.

"Information about Russians," he said.

"Do you mean my friends?"

"Yes, anybody."

Zhanna felt a sudden sickness in the pit of her stomach. It was informants who had brought Stalin's secret police to their home in Berdyansk to arrest her father. Informants who had directed Jew-hunting Nazis to the family's apartment in Kharkov. Informants who had told the Germans that Anna and Marina were Jews. She could not, would not, do this.

Zhanna burst into tears. The young interrogator, panicked at the sight of a young woman crying, rushed around the table and tried to comfort Zhanna.

"What have I done?" he asked, puzzled.

Zhanna wiped her tears, steadied herself, and looked him in the eye.

"I did not go through war and lying for five years to become a spy on my friends. My father told me *never* to spy on anybody."

The young man put away his pen and notebook. "That's all right," he said softly. "I would never ask you to betray your father."

So Zhanna's career as an informant ended before it even began. She and Frina had now been at Funk Kaserne for almost a year—an eternity of rutabaga soup and French housekeeping.

"You know," Larry said one day, "you've got to leave this place. Where would you like to go? England? France?"

They had no idea. The options were bewildering. But they had one thing in common—no connection to the girls' past, to the world as they knew it. All that Zhanna and Frina knew for sure was that they were never going home.

Chapter Twenty-Three

Many women lost their husbands to the war—the lucky ones, only temporarily. A few, like Grace Dawson, lost them to the peace. Mustering supplies and running a motor pool in West Palm Beach had not satisfied 2nd Lieutenant Laurence A. Dawson's urge to serve his country in war. Probably the greatest danger he faced in three years was a high inside fastball in the baseball games the military posts organized to pass the time. Larry had enough time left over to write long, rambling letters to David with inning-by-inning descriptions of games, with complete box scores.

"We played the 22nd last Friday," he wrote in August 1943. "They were the best hitters we've seen yet. But we beat them 5-1. The answer was Stewart, our new pitcher. He is a quiet little New Englander, about 5ft, 5in, and weighing 145. And he wears glasses. He looked like a sissy or a scholar, but the players on the 22nd call him far and away the best they've seen in the league, and admitted frankly they were scared at the plate. For my part, I got no hits, but was not dissatisfied because I hit two balls plenty hard. One was a double I got robbed of. The other was a red-hot line smash to the shortstop. I fouled out once on a pop-up. Well, that's about all the story of that game. Tomorrow we play the 313th, and the odds are all against us. In starting Lefty Harrick we are taking a chance on an aging pitcher against a team which in 5 games has never scored less than 7 runs per game. So long. I'll write you a long letter if we win tomorrow and a short one if we lose."

As soon as the war ended, Larry volunteered with the United Nations Relief and Rehabilitation Administration (UNRRA) and left for Germany to be head of the displaced persons camp at Funk Kaserne, where he would later meet Zhanna and Frina. Grace went home to Virginia with two-year-old Lad to await the birth of their second child, and to wonder when her husband would return so they could resume a normal life. She was patient. Grace understood Larry's need to go, and felt the fulfillment in his letters from Germany. He told her about the Latvian and Lithuanian refugees he had rescued from Soviet thugs, and about sheltering others who came to him and said they would rather face a firing squad at Funk Kaserne than be taken "home" by Soviet agents.

"He told me how these people were so grateful to him for what he did, that so many of them had brought him gifts, and I realized that he was doing a really big job as head of the camp."

Grace was well acquainted with the deep quixotic streak in Larry, never surprised by the latest windmill in his sights, but she was not prepared for the letter she received in early 1946.

"He said there were two teenage girls in the camp that were great pianists. He thought they were better pianists than probably anybody at the Juilliard School of Music, and he thought that's where they ought to be, but he had no way of getting them a visa. He had looked into every different idea and the best chance of getting them to the United States was if we adopted them."

Grace took a deep breath. Lad was 2½. George—whose tardy birth she induced with castor oil—was just an infant, and they were all living with Grace's parents because the farmhouse she and Larry purchased before the war still had no electricity or plumbing. There was no room for two more children, almost fully grown. And what if Larry was wrong about the girls' talent? What if he knew as little about music as he did about farming?

"I was thinking about what would happen if they didn't get into Juilliard," Grace said. "But Larry was sure he could get them in, and I was inclined to believe him because he could do pretty much what he wanted to do, and he had a lot of pull and all kinds of guts about trying. So I agreed if that's what he wanted to do, I would go along with it."

Bringing Zhanna and Frina to America was not Larry's first thought when the war ended. He thought they would be happier in Europe, close to their homeland, even if they never went back. Larry went through a list of likely destinations with the girls.

> It was kind of a given that we would continue our music. We considered England and France but thought the spirit would be gloomy after all the destruction of war. We thought the same about Italy in spite of its gorgeous musical tradition. No country had a greater musical history than Germany, but we could not go there. It would be like going back to a place where you had been beaten up and robbed. We were at a dead end.

Larry realized that the process of elimination pointed inescapably in one direction.

"Would you like to go to America?" he asked.

Zhanna hesitated. She thought Larry was kidding, but she didn't dare say so in case he was serious. America existed in Russian minds as a fairytale, a wonderland where they make movies and have no wars and there is chocolate for everyone.

"Who *wouldn't* want to go to America?" Zhanna told Larry.

Larry soon discovered that fulfilling the girls' fantasy would be easier said than done. "There might be trouble," he reported to the girls. "I don't know if I can do it."

U.S. immigration laws in 1946 were draconian, a sobering asterisk to the Statue of Liberty's open invitation to the tired and the poor. The annual immigration quota for all central and eastern European countries was 39,000, and two thirds of that was allotted to Germany. The law was hopelessly inadequate to deal with millions of displaced persons in post war Europe.

In December 1945, President Truman ordered special measures to speed up the flow of refugees to the United States, with preference given to orphans and adults with relatives in the U.S. Truman's directive stated that the immigrants or their families would be responsible for visa fees and travel fare, and that any refugees "likely to become public charges"—go on welfare—would be turned away.

With no money and no relatives in the U.S., Zhanna and Frina were not ideal candidates for immigration. The only person they knew with a relative in America was Regina Horowitz, their ensemble teacher at the Kharkov conservatory, and sister of legendary pianist Vladimir Horowitz—not a likely guardian for two ragged refugees, even if they were fellow Ukrainian pianists.

Larry worked the immigration bureaucracy for months but could not get around the fact there was no quota for Russian Jews. The only solution was to adopt the girls, giving them automatic preference. Larry thought he could pull enough strings to get it done, but there still was the matter of visa fees and travel fares, and he already was sending as much money home to Grace as he could. Larry's UNRRA colleagues set up a fund to get the girls to America. His best friend, Ed Savage—a shy, handsome G.I. both sisters liked—gave $2,000, a princely sum in 1945, on the condition Larry keep it secret because Ed didn't want the girls to feel obligated.

Finally, the plans were set. In late April, the girls would go to Bremen in northern Germany for processing of papers, then on to the North Sea port of Bremerhaven for departure. Larry feared the plans could be torpedoed by legalities and red tape— a reasonable fear since he had not yet officially adopted the girls. In the meantime, however, Zhanna had turned eighteen, making it legally possible for her to accompany Frina, still considered a child at sixteen.

Larry was sending the girls into a legal minefield, and he would not be there to guide them. Unable to leave his UNRRA duties in Munich, he had a member of his staff drive the girls to Bremen. On April 29, Larry wrote to his brother, David, and Paul Magriel, a ballet critic and friend in New York. He hoped that one or both would meet the girls when their boat docked.

"Yesterday, the two Russian Jewish orphan girls left Funk

Kaserne for Bremen on the first leg of their journey to the USA as emigrants. Unless they are detained at Bremen, which is quite possible for a number of reasons, they should sail about May 8th and reach New York shortly after the middle of the month.

"They carry with them a letter from Grace stating that she wishes to adopt them both, and a letter from me to the U.S. Committee for the Care of European Children. All child emigrants technically come under the supervision of the Committee, and it is quite possible the Committee will try to exercise its jurisdiction and pick their home for them. I would like to ask you both to do everything necessary to see to it that these kids go to me.

"That will, first, consist of convincing the Committee that my home is a good one for them. I own a sizeable house and 108 acres of fine farmland. This will be completely paid for by September. My country home will be an ideal milieu for them. Due to a remarkable interest in these girls by one of my officers here, I will have $2,400 to be used for them at my discretion.

"There is another thing I would like to emphasize to the Committee: these girls are promising music students, and in entering my family they will be in a musical atmosphere. It is important to point out David's standing as a well-known professional musician and to say that his assistance in helping guide their musical education will be a big thing."

Larry neglected to mention that his farmhouse surely was the only one in Crozet—likely all of Virginia—with a Steinway grand piano in the living room. It was a gift from his Aunt Marian in Bethesda, Maryland, who had owned it since she was a young woman but never learned to play. After Larry left for

Europe, the piano sat alone for years in the vacant, unheated farmhouse—an unseemly fate for such a fine instrument. But now, with Zhanna and Frina on the way, Aunt Marian's gift seemed providential.

David, too, had joined the service in 1943, and like many musicians was assigned to duty in the states, playing in War Bond Concerts and at military posts. After being honorably discharged in 1946, he joined the Gordon String Quartet and was on tour when Larry wrote to him about the girls. David was eager to help. In 1939, he had played in a benefit concert for German Jewish refugees at The Hebrew Free School in New York—Jews lucky or prescient enough to have fled before the war. Here was an opportunity to help two others who had not been so fortunate. And Larry's description of the girls had piqued his curiosity.

"The girls speak Russian, bad German, and very, very little English," he wrote. "They are the two most lovable kids any of us here have ever known. We have never seen any other DPs who have been through what they have and who retain a pure, fresh, uncynical attitude toward, and faith in, life. They have seen the filthiest and worst things in Europe and come through it pure as gold. I hope you will get to know them. Then you will realize why six of us moved heaven and Earth to get them to America."

None of Larry's worst bureaucratic fears materialized at Bremen. The girls breezed through the immigration checkpoint and were added to the passenger list of the S.S. *Marine Flasher*, a converted army troop ship scheduled to take the first boatload of Holocaust survivors to America.

On May 11, 1946, Larry wrote to David.

"The two Jewish orphans Grace and I are going to adopt—Janna and Frina Arschanskaja—sailed today for America and will reach NY about the 20th of the month. It is, of course, very important that someone meet the girls at the boat. Keep in touch with Grace, who knows all about it, naturally. The kids will wear something white around their left arms at the pier to help you identify them. They are extremely short on clothes, since getting clothes in Germany today is next to impossible, so their appearance will probably be a bit shabby."

Larry also felt obliged to lower expectations about the girls' musical talent which he feared he had praised to unreasonable heights with his talk of Juilliard.

"You will notice many big faults in their playing," he wrote to David. "You should remember they have heard almost no music. They were displaced by the war when they were very small, and so their comprehension of music is purely innate, not developed at all by experience. I have coached them a lot myself. Four months ago they had almost no sense of rhythm and they 'banged' out everything. Their progress in four months has been tremendous, especially for the younger of the two, who four months ago was not recognizable as a pianist in any sense."

The Herculean extent of Larry's string-pulling to get Zhanna and Frina on the S.S. *Marine Flasher* was evident in this fact: among the approximately eight hundred Jews on board, they were the only Russians. Most were Polish, with a sprinkling from fifteen other nationalities.

·

Larry thought because of us the boat might be turned around. He told us repeatedly, "Not until you are very far out on the ocean can you be sure that you are on the way to America. They can return you any time." We were very nervous. How would we know by looking at the water when we were safe?

Thankfully, Zhanna and Frina knew nothing of the ignominious affair that haunted Larry and triggered his repeated warning, which had begun to sound like an eerie prophesy. The S.S. *Marine Flasher* was leaving for America almost seven years to the day—May 13, 1939—that the S.S. *St. Louis* departed Hamburg for Havana carrying nearly a thousand Jews in search of refuge from Hitler. The *St. Louis* was turned away by Cuba and the U.S.—a floating pariah—and forced to return to Germany, where many of the passengers perished in the Holocaust. It became known as The Voyage of the Damned.

Zhanna and Frina each carried a small leather suitcase and an accordion onto the boat. Zhanna had two other possessions. One was a blue concert dress she bought in Kremenchug with bottles of vodka lavished on her by giddy German soldiers who loved Grieg and Schubert more than they loved their Führer. The other—her most precious possession—was her tattered copy of *Fantasy Impromptu.*

She reached inside her coat, as she had a thousand times before, and felt for the sheet music—five pages with a sketch of Chopin on the front—which she salvaged from her home in Kharkov the day the Nazis took them away to Drobitsky Yar. But she was not thinking of that terrible day now. She was thinking of a night in Berdyansk long ago, of her father and Nicoli playing Verdi and Rossini overtures by candlelight in the living room as she drifted off to sleep. Those ancient lullabies decorated her dreams as the S.S. *Marine Flasher* churned west, away from darkness into the light, toward the deeper, safer water Larry talked about. Toward America.

Chapter Twenty-Four

The S.S. *Marine Flasher* was a troop transport built to carry soldiers to war, not a cruise ship designed with the comfort and pleasure of vacationers in mind. But to Zhanna and Frina it felt like the *Queen Mary*. They had their own tiny cabin—a luxury after years of communal bedrooms—and what seemed to be a nonstop feast.

There was no end to it—piles of food! And so much superior to what we ate for years. It was the first time I saw a banana. I couldn't understand why it was black. I opened it up and it was white and sweet—very nice. Frina and I just kept stuffing ourselves and the more we ate, the worse we felt, especially me. There were no pills for nausea. It was horrible.

But worse than seasickness was the pain of rejection by their fellow passengers and Holocaust survivors. The Poles treated the sisters as if they were carriers of a deadly contagious disease. What a cruel irony, Zhanna thought, that on this voyage to a new land that worshipped the future, they were victims of enmities rooted in the distant past.

Poles hated Russians more than anyone on Earth.
Russia was the big, dominating neighbor. And Poles
always considered themselves the aristocracy of Europe,
totally Western. The Russians were strictly Eastern—
savages. The Poles were outraged we were on the
boat. They said we were stupid to be going to America
without any family there. They wanted to prove they
were the chosen ones and that we were impostors.

The sisters did not make a single acquaintance on the voyage. Even their accordions won them no friends on a boat full of bored people starved for diversion. Their ostracism was total. It took nine days to cross the Atlantic, but for Zhanna, beset by nausea and boredom and the ill will of her fellow travelers, it seemed like nine years.

On the morning of May 20, Zhanna was awakened by shouts and excited cries from outside. She bolted out of her cabin up a narrow set of steel steps to the main deck and looked west. Stretching across the horizon behind a scrim of early-morning haze was a frieze of dramatic stiletto peaks like an irregular heartbeat.

America!

Zhanna and Frina found spots on the crowded rail near the bow and watched in awestruck silence as the S.S. *Marine Flasher* sailed up New York Bay, past the Statue of Liberty and Ellis Island—by then used only for detention of alien enemies—up the Hudson River past lower Manhattan before docking at Pier 64 just south of West 33rd Street. Waiting on the pier was a huge crowd of friends, relatives, members of the press, and officials of various immigration agencies. Some older passengers wept, others waved joyously as they recognized a face in the crowd, or saw their name on a hand-lettered sign.

Zhanna scanned the sea of faces and wondered which one was David, Larry's younger brother, the gifted violist they had heard so much about. Larry promised he would be there to meet them. On May 15, Larry sent a telegram to remind David: "JANNA AND FRIENA ARRIVE NEWYORK ABOUT MAY TWENTIETH ABOARD MARINE FLASHER BE SURE TO MEET THEM."

The sisters put on the white arm bands Larry had fashioned for them out of an old bed sheet and gathered up their belongings. With suitcases and accordions in hand, they made their way slowly down the gangplank and waded into the crowd. All around them, people were laughing and embracing and posing for photos. Some of the immigrants were being interviewed by members of the press. Any moment now, Zhanna thought, David would rush up to them and *their* celebration would begin.

But no one rushed up to embrace them. They stood conspicuously alone on the pier, the only immigrants not surrounded by family or friends. No one even bothered to ask if they needed help. Soon the pier was deserted, an empty ballroom after New Year's Eve. Eventually, a dock worker took the girls to an office where they waited like children who had become separated from their parents in a department store. Zhanna was still fighting waves of nausea from the voyage. They had no money, no one to call, nowhere to go.

Where was David? Where was *anybody?*

Finally, a solitary person appeared from nowhere looking for us. He said his name was Paul and he showed us a telegram from David asking him to meet us. Paul spoke a little German, like us, and it took a long time for us to understand exactly who he was and why David wasn't there.

David, on tour with the Gordon String Quartet, could not get away and had recruited Paul Magriel, a good friend, to meet the girls when they arrived. No one on the pier was very happy about the change in plans.

We were tremendously disappointed. And Paul didn't seem very uplifted by the sight of us. In my eyes he kind of blended in with the rest of the colorless surroundings of Pier 64. No one tried to show much enthusiasm or charm.

The girls' first day in America was proving to be a dud. The sullen trio had a few hours to kill before the girls boarded a train at Grand Central Station for Crozet, near Charlottesville. In her broken German, Zhanna explained to Paul that there was something she needed before getting on the train—a Russian-to-English dictionary. Her impression of New York improved as they walked east on 33rd Street to Fifth Avenue and the shadow of the Empire State Building. Paul took them up Fifth Avenue past store windows in which they saw beautiful things and their own ragged reflections. Finally, they came to a bookstore, the largest and finest Zhanna had ever seen.

Paul took out his wallet and gestured that he would pay for the book. He explained to a clerk, a middle-aged man, what Zhanna wanted. She was startled when the clerk turned to her and spoke in Russian.

"I don't understand why you came to this country," he said. Zhanna could tell by his accent that he was Russian, perhaps the son of earlier immigrants, not a Russian-speaking American.

"We had no choice," she said. "The Germans killed our parents. We had no other place to go."

The clerk shook his head. "This is a very bad mistake—you will not like it here."

Zhanna was rattled by her fellow Russian's insolence and negative manner. There was a choice Russian word for people like him, but she couldn't find it in her new dictionary. Maybe the English are too polite to use that word, she thought.

Paul found a quick antidote to the clerk's sour pessimism—a place that embodied the outsized appetites, abundance, and entrepreneurial spirit which made America a seductive beacon to the dispossessed around the world: Woolworth's Five and Dime. One look inside the cavernous temple of tchotchkes and the sisters' gloom vanished.

It was absolutely beautiful. We were mesmerized by all the jewelry and other cheap items—by the sparkle and organization. We thought it was the best store in the world.

For Zhanna, now nineteen, it was more than that. It was a doorway back to a lost childhood—the price she had paid for survival. The war had made her grow up before her time. Wandering wide-eyed through the aisles of the dime-store palace on Fifth Avenue, she was transported back in time. She was in Berdyansk again, a barefoot urchin exploring the bazaars and apothecary shops of her beloved seaside home. Zhanna had no money, but there was nothing she wanted to buy at Woolworth. She just wanted to look, to revel in a resurrected joy she thought had been buried forever at Drobitsky Yar.

At Grand Central, Paul bought the girls a box of chocolates and gave them taxi fare and a note from Larry explaining who they were and how to get to the farmhouse in Crozet which Grace and her father had been renovating in his absence. Paul told the conductor the girls did not speak English and, slipping him a dollar, said to make sure they got off at Crozet.

This was the girls' first train trip since the hellish evacuation from Berlin to Bavaria when they were spat on and called vile names by German civilians who would have choked them if they had been able to move their arms in the packed car. Now, as the train wended its way south through Pennsylvania and Maryland, late afternoon fading to dusk then darkness, the girls' lingering trauma succumbed to the metronomic rocking of the cars and to their own deep exhaustion.

We had not eaten all day, but we were more tired than hungry. We put the candy on our laps and started eating it, and before we knew it we were asleep. We slept soundly.

Almost too soundly. It was pitch-black outside when the girls were jolted awake by the hysterical voice of the conductor.

"Crozet! Crozet! Get up! It's time for you to get off the train!"

Groggy and disoriented, the girls scrambled out of their seats. Chocolates went flying in all directions. They grabbed their suitcases and accordions and stumbled down the steps of the train. A single light burned in the tiny Crozet station. They handed Larry's note to the clerk who called a cab. Using his hands and shouting in English, the driver indicated it would take twenty to thirty minutes to reach Larry's farmhouse. The cab plunged into the inky blackness of the Virginia countryside.

All we had was the narrow vision of the car's headlights. I will never forget the aroma of thick, lush greenery. It was the first time in my life I smelled honeysuckle. It was so wonderful—it filled the car.

As the driver, predicted, had minutes later the cab pulled up to Larry's farmhouse. The house was dark, not surprising considering the late hour. The driver waited as the girls knocked on the door. Once, twice, three times. No answer. They glanced in a window—the house appeared empty, except for a large shape Zhanna could not make out. She cupped her hands around her eyes and squinted.

"It's a piano!" she said. "Only Larry could live here."

But no one was living there yet. Apparently, the renovation was not finished. "What now?" Zhanna thought, surveying the desolate scene. Luckily, Larry had considered the possibility that the driver would not be able to find the farmhouse, and had instructed him in the note to ask directions to the home of George Jarman, Grace's father. This was easier said than done after midnight in rural Virginia where farmers are in bed by nine. A cold rain had begun to fall, further cutting visibility.

The Jarman home was only six miles from Larry's, but it took the driver ninety minutes of meandering and asking directions to find it. The home was situated fifty yards off the highway at the end of a dirt road which had turned to mud in the cold spring rain. Once again, the driver waited as the girls approached a darkened house. Unlike the first stop, this was a full house: Grace, her sons Lad and George, her mother and father, and two boys her parents were raising, almost as foster sons.

Grace was the first to hear the knocking. She awoke with a start. Something's happened to Larry, she thought. They're here to tell me. Who else would come this far out in the country after midnight?

She threw on a housecoat and went to the door, her heart pounding. There was no window to look out so she opened the door a crack and saw two shadowy figures on the porch. Thank God, she thought, they are not wearing military uniforms. Her second thought: It must be the girls Larry is sending. But they weren't supposed to be there yet. As far as she knew, Larry had not even gotten visas for the girls. She opened the door wide.

"You are Grace?" Zhanna asked in English.

"Yes," Grace said. "Come in out of the rain."

The girls were soaking wet. Their leather suitcases gave off a terrible smell, and Grace noticed they walked oddly as if their shoes didn't fit.

Grace saw the headlights of the taxi at the end of the road. The driver was standing by the car waiting to make sure this, finally, was the right house. It was two hours since he had picked up the girls at the station.

"Thank you very much!" Grace called out. "What do I owe you for bringing the girls?"

"No, ma'am, nothing," he said. "I'm doing this. This is on me."

There were awkward "hellos" through the language barrier and bleary eyes. Grace gave the girls towels to dry off. She offered them ham and biscuits and cold milk, which they eagerly devoured. Finally, after a day that had begun in the canyons of Manhattan and ended in the foothills of the Blue Ridge Mountains, it was time for sleep.

There were two double beds with feather mattresses in the downstairs bedroom. Zhanna shared one bed with Grace and 2 ½-year-old Lad. Frina slept in the other with Grace's mother. Five-month-old George was in a crib next to Grace's bed. The room was cold, but it was warm under the homemade quilts.

Zhanna and Frina were used to sharing beds with strangers. This night was no different in that way from so many others in their long odyssey. Every night in a strange bed had been followed the next day by the search for another place of refuge. But this night was different, too. The running and hiding and searching had finally come to an end, here in the honeysuckle darkness of Virginia.

This night was unlike any that Zhanna and Frina had ever known because of its tomorrow. Tomorrow would be their first morning in America.

Chapter Twenty-Five

The late-night excitement did not alter the rhythms of life on the Jarman farm. Grace was up before dawn, as usual, and gave Zhanna and Frina only a few extra minutes before politely rousting them out of bed. She did give them a reprieve from chores on their first morning. The first cow-milking lesson could wait a day.

Dressed in their same road-weary outfits, the girls sat down at the long kitchen table for breakfast, grateful for the warmth of the wood-burning stove. Grace tried to introduce them to the rest of the curious family. The language barrier produced lots of smiles and little conversation.

We were presented with a big, deep bowl of oatmeal.
We had never seen anything like that in Russia.
It was totally tasteless. There was just one other thing,
a plate of bacon, kind of burned. It was so salty we
couldn't eat it.

Grace was still wondering why Larry had not written to let her know that Zhanna and Frina would be showing up on her doorstep any day. On the other hand, given the Dawson propensity for absent-mindedness and procrastination, why was she surprised? In any case, the surprise arrival meant that Grace and her boys and Zhanna and Frina would have to move to the farmhouse right away, even though the renovation was not complete. There simply wasn't room in the Jarman house for nine people.

But the most pressing task was to get the girls some shoes that fit. Each had arrived at the farm with four pairs of shoes, given to them at Funk Kaserne, and none fit. After breakfast, Grace loaded them into the Jarmans' old car and took them into Charlottesville. The first stop was a shoe store. The girls had never seen one, and were amused by the idea of a shoe salesman. A man kneeling to put a shoe on a woman's foot! Such things happened only in fairytales about princes and glass slippers.

They giggled as the salesman placed their feet in the metal measuring device and slid the bar up and down. Little wonder they had been walking awkwardly. He discovered that their old shoes were two sizes too small. The girls quickly adapted to American ways, trying on many pairs of shoes. Each left with a pair of saddle oxfords. It was the first time they could remember their feet not hurting. Next was a clothing store where Grace bought them skirts and blouses. She figured the girls would attend the local high school, at least until Larry returned from Europe, and they had nothing resembling school clothes.

The last stop was the soda fountain at Timberlake's drug Store. Its wide array of ice cream treats was another new concept to the girls. There was ice cream in Russia, wonderful ice cream from the freshest cream, but it was only sold from carts on the street. A warm vanilla aroma enveloped the girls as they stepped inside the store. There were customers sitting at tables with round backless stools covered in shiny red vinyl. Behind the counter a pony-tailed girl pulled on a lever and frothy brown liquid streamed into tall glasses marked "Coca-Cola"—two of the words in their limited English vocabularies. They could not read the menu on the wall offering cones, shakes, sundaes, and a variety of flavors, so Grace ordered for them. The man behind the counter in a funny paper cap looked at the girls then winked at Grace.

After a few minutes he appeared holding two mountainous banana splits—three scoops of ice cream, three kinds of syrup, nuts, whipped cream, and a cherry on top. The girls' eyes were like saucers. But when the glass dishes were placed on the table before them, they just stared. They didn't know how to eat a banana split. Grace had to take a spoon and demonstrate. Their first bites released a torrent of excited Russian, then an international language.

"*Mmmmm . . . mmmm!*"

Other customers in the parlor, overhearing the oddly-accented shrieks of pleasure, moved closer for a better look. Grace had to tell them something.

"These Russian girls just came from Germany by boat and were met in New York and came by train to Crozet in the middle of the night and took a taxi to our farm," she said. "They didn't have any shoes that fit them and we had to come shopping, and they never had a banana split before. Does anyone here speak Russian?"

There was applause, but no hands went up. The girls scraped the bottom of the dishes with their spoons to get the last bits of whipped cream and chocolate. Grace went to the counter to pay, but as she reached into her wallet a customer walked up and put a hand on her arm.

"Let me get it," said the man in a business suit. "Tell them it's my way of saying welcome to America."

Sorry, Grace said, but she didn't know how to tell them that. The man turned to Zhanna and spoke in the overly deliberate way Americans address anyone who doesn't speak English.

"What . . . is . . . your . . . *name?*"

Zhanna had heard the question often enough over the past five years to understand it and answer it in several languages. She was thankful that she no longer had to stop and think about the answer, that at last she was in a place where she never again would have to lie, never again have to disown the name and memory of her mother and father simply to survive. Smiling broadly, she extended her hand to the American.

"My name is Zhanna Arshanskaya!"

Chapter Twenty-Six

Zhanna had survived bombs and the Holocaust, but there were days she wondered if she would survive life on the Dawson farm. This was the hardest work she had ever done. Yes, as a child she had spent hours a day at the piano bench mastering keyboard technique and classical repertory under the demanding ear of her father and leading piano pedagogues in the Soviet Union. And after the war she had endured the most severe taskmaster of all, Larry, who pushed her and Frina to performance heights like a jockey whipping a thoroughbred down the homestretch.

But farming was different. There were no shouts of "Bravo!" after she milked the cow. No standing ovations for hours spent in the garden weeding and picking berries. No glowing newspaper reviews for firing up the wood stove in the morning, fixing breakfast, and cleaning up. No smitten soldiers coming to her window with flowers and cakes and bottles of schnapps. And there was another critical difference.

Zhanna loved music, which mitigated the tedium of daily practice required of a piano virtuoso. She did *not* love farming. When she was little, Zhanna helped her mother can vegetables and fruit from their backyard garden in Berdyansk, but that was a lark. She spent most of her time exploring the town. Her only real manual labor was at the keyboard.

Grace had grown up on a farm doing every sort of manual labor and learning the skills essential to subsistence farming. She was handy but had only two hands, and with two young children, a farm to run, and Larry in Europe, she needed all the help she could get. She worked hard and expected the same of Zhanna and Frina.

On the cold, rainy night the girls arrived from New York, Grace was still living at her parents' home, awaiting renovation of the farmhouse she and Larry had bought before he left for Europe. The Jarman home was not large enough for the suddenly expanded family, nine including Zhanna and Frina, to comfortably coexist. A few days later Grace moved the girls and her boys to the farmhouse even though it still lacked electricity and plumbing—not uncommon for an old farmhouse of the day—and everyone was forced to make do.

Grace, her father George, and a helper immediately went to work adding creature comforts to the house. Larry "never knew how to drive a nail straight," she said, so he wasn't missed. In truth, his absence was almost a relief since Larry had the maddening habit of sitting in front of the radio listening to baseball games, oblivious to Grace laboring in the background. It was even worse when Larry's younger brother, David, a musician with similar hammering skills, came to visit, and Grace had to listen to their arguing and laughter as she toiled. The renovation was proceeding much better without their "help."

"There was an old colored man, a handyman, working with

my father," Grace said. "We were putting in water and electricity and a bathroom. We had to use a pot before we got the thing finished. There was an outhouse for daytime, but at night you had a slop bucket. You'd have a utensil and take it out and empty it every day, and that was the way you lived on the farm."

With Grace doing skilled labor, the brunt of domestic duties fell on Zhanna, now nineteen, and Frina, seventeen. They cooked, they cleaned, they looked after the boys. They were miserable. Their father had trained them for the concert hall, not the barnyard. They daydreamed of running away and going back to Russia. But they never spoke of it—or, Grace noticed, about the war. Her gentle, tentative probing on the subject invariably was rebuffed by silence.

"The language barrier was a problem for deep conversation, but they did not seem to want to talk about it at all," Grace said. "They were very secretive. They seemed frightened to talk about it, as if they were afraid someone would come after them."

Grace was wrong. The fear Zhanna carried with her for five years now lay somewhere on the bottom of the Atlantic. She had mentally dumped it overboard when finally she was certain the *Marine Flasher* would not—as Larry warned might happen— reverse course and return her and Frina to their tormentors. Zhanna *chose* not to speak of the war. What was there to say? They had survived. She thought of it often, though. How could she not? She was reminded each time she opened her dresser drawer and noticed, beneath her things, the *Fantasy Impromptu* sheet music Professor Luntz had given her, which she had so painstakingly preserved and transported during the war.

Soon after the girls arrived, Grace had enrolled them in

Greenwood High School, which was situated near Crozet in the foothills of the Blue Ridge Mountains and had a senior class of about forty. It was a doomed experiment. The sisters were there two weeks, but to Zhanna it felt like two months.

We wasted our time. We were bored to tears. There was no studying, absolutely no knowledge. They were telling us how to put something together in the kitchen. Home economics. This was unheard of in Russian schools. In Russia, I already had biology and algebra by fourth grade. There were a lot of lectures, and questions and answers. In this school we were just staring at them and they were looking at us. They should have found someone to teach us English. We were outraged. This was a school?

The first time Zhanna heard English spoken in Europe after the war she thought it was a joke—surely not a real language—and she had not changed her opinion since arriving in America.

There were so many things I could not absorb, like the word "under" as compared to "over." So, I wrote on the inside of my forearm "under" and "over" on the top of it.

Even worse for Zhanna and Frina than the stout language barrier was the cultural isolation of tiny Crozet. For the first time in their lives, including the war, the sisters were almost totally cut off from music and musicians. The only bridge to that life was the Steinway grand which sat incongruously in the front room of the farmhouse. Larry's Aunt Marian, no longer having use for it in her Bethesda, Maryland, home, had given him the piano and it sat for two years in the vacant, unheated farmhouse.

To some, the rendezvous of a Steinway grand and two Holocaust survivors in a farmhouse in rural Virginia might seem providential. To Zhanna and Frina, it simply helped make farm life bearable. Each managed to practice an hour or two a day amid the household din. Sometimes this meant staying up late to complete farm chores, but it was worth losing sleep to be ready for an audition that could be their ticket out of Crozet back into the musical life. Meanwhile, the piano managed to poke a hole in the language barrier.

"Lad was about 2½ when the girls came," Grace said. "The fact they couldn't speak English didn't matter 'cause they just talked to the boys in Russian. Lad learned to speak Russian before he learned English. We'd have a song night where they played the piano and he'd do these little songs they taught him in Russian."

Little "Georgie," as the girls called him, was too young for sing-alongs, but every morning at six they would load him in his buggy for the mile-and-a-half stroll to a country store where each girl handed over a nickel for a Clark Bar. They had been introduced to the Clark Bar by an American in Europe. The honeycomb peanut crisp bar with a chocolate coating was both a revelation and a curiosity to the sisters. There were no candy bars in Russia, and almost no candy was sold in a wrapper, including the caramels produced by Zhanna's father Dmitri, a master candy maker. Paper was a scarce, precious commodity in

Ukraine. What idiot would put a wrapper on something when people eat it *without* paper? Zhanna wondered.

After a few months of daily Clark Bars, Zhanna looked in the mirror and wondered who that pimply, round-faced girl was, frowning back at her. Where was the slim Ukrainian beauty with flawless almond skin? This plump imposter was also constipated. It wasn't just the Clark Bars, it was a diet light on green vegetables and heavy on potatoes, bread, oatmeal, and fried apples—a diet better suited to a farm hand than a pianist. Occasionally the girls would fix a pot of borscht with cabbage and beets, using their mother's recipe.

> *One of my big disappointments was the food. The cow*
> *produced milk full of onion smell and I could not drink*
> *it. We had cereal and enough bread and potatoes. There*
> *was a lot of bacon grease on the stove and we thought it*
> *would taste good to fry the apples in the bacon grease. I*
> *turned into an ugly, horrible little thing with pimples.*
> *I became constipated forever. You could not unconstipate*
> *me.*

A visit to the doctor revealed that Zhanna had packed an extra twentyfive pounds on her delicate five-foot-four frame. He told her to choose between potatoes and bread, and to cut down on the apples fried in bacon grease. She followed the doctor's orders with the discipline of a performer, and soon the pimply, fat-faced girl in the mirror was just an ugly memory. The Ukrainian beauty had returned, just in time.

One day in late October, Grace told the girls they were taking a trip to Washington, D.C., to hear Larry's brother, David, perform with the Gordon String Quartet. Zhanna nearly wept with joy. To be escaping the farm for a concert was a double deliverance from the physical and cultural isolation of Crozet which had driven her to near depression and too many fried apples. The fact they were going to hear the legendary David lent special excitement to the occasion.

> *Larry never stopped talking about David. He was so proud to have a professional musician in the family. He loved David so much. He was his biggest buddy in life.*

David and Zhanna were fellow prodigies in parallel worlds separated by fourteen years, eight thousand miles and dramatically opposite twists of fate. David, who earned comparisons to Mozart for his precocious musicality, had left his hometown of Charlottesville, Virginia, for the Juilliard School of Music at age fourteen. The same year, 1927, Zhanna was born in Berdyansk in southern Ukraine. Like David, she left home at age fourteen, but she did it at the point of a Nazi gun, not for a scholarship. At Juilliard, David's teacher, Hans Letz, persuaded him to switch from violin to viola to take advantage of his large hands and long, supple fingers—a wise insight that catapulted David to the rarefied heights of his profession.

His first job after graduating from Juilliard at twenty two was in the Metropolitan Opera Orchestra. He played in orchestras for Broadway musicals and the studio orchestra for the Burns and Allen radio show, and was in the first traveling production of *Porgy and Bess,* taking George Gershwin's money in poker games on long train rides between cities. He spent three years as principal viola of the Minneapolis Symphony under the baton of Dimitri Mitropoulos; then, following his musical heart, joined the Coolidge String Quartet. The quartet was on tour in 1943 when Uncle Sam decided he wanted David to play in War Bond Concerts and entertain the troops on military installations in the U.S.—just as Zhanna had been "drafted" by the Führer to entertain his soldiers and slave workers. After the war, David joined the celebrated Gordon String Quartet formed in 1921 by Russian-born violinist Jacques Gordon, who was appointed concertmaster of the Chicago Symphony the same year. Gordon divided his time and affections before leaving the symphony in 1930 to devote full time to the quartet and his solo career. He established a summer residence for the quartet on a remote hilltop in the southern Berkshires and called it Music Mountain. It was a transcendent setting for chamber music, and David, a romantic, immediately fell under its spell.

Zhanna didn't know any of this about David, or much else in terms of his temperament, because Larry usually spoke only in broad superlatives about his little brother's musical virtuosity. Zhanna's keen anticipation of meeting David—a small gathering was planned after the concert—was thus wrapped in mystery. Grace, however, had provided an intriguing glimpse of the person behind the viola.

> *She said that while Larry wasn't a good farmer, in comparison to David he was excellent! She told us he was totally different from Larry in other ways, an ultra-sophisticated, big-town musician who wore*

patent-leather shoes. In Russia it is a tradition to wear
these kinds of shoes at formal concerts, so we had a
picture of David as very formal person. We were going
to find out if this was true.

Zhanna had hours to speculate as Grace steered the family's old DeSoto northeast from Charlottesville on U.S. Route 29 to Pratts and Culpeper and Nokesville, on through Manassas to Washington, D.C.—a journey of 120 miles, winding but lovely, for autumn was applying its final brilliant brushstrokes to the Virginia countryside. Zhanna was transfixed. The train ride from New York to Crozet had been in darkness. This was her first look at the American countryside in the light of day.

The towering edifices of Fifth Avenue had not prepared Zhanna for the beauty of Washington, its breathtaking fusion of sylvan splendor and grandeur. Grace took them first to the Lincoln Memorial, an iconic image even in Soviet textbooks. From there they walked east along the Reflecting Pool, past the Washington Monument and the length of the Mall to the steps of the Capitol. Just beyond the Capitol on Independence Avenue they saw the Thomas Jefferson Building, one of three buildings housing the Library of Congress. The Jefferson is an ornate Italian Renaissance revival with white marble floors and columns, two grand staircases, vaulted ceilings, and a gold-plated dome. On the ground floor is the Coolidge Auditorium—the visitors' ultimate destination that day.

Elizabeth Sprague Coolidge, a wealthy patroness of music, donated $60,000 in 1924 for construction of an auditorium to serve as a permanent stage for chamber music concerts and the performance of compositions she commissioned from a Who's Who of twentieth century musical genius including Bela Bartok, Paul Hindemith, Sergei Prokofiev, Maurice Ravel, Igor Stravinsky, Arnold Schoenberg, and Aaron Copland, whose *Appalachian Spring* ballet had its 1944 premiere in the Coolidge Auditorium. The Gordon Quartet had performed many times in the 485-seat auditorium, revered by chamber music players for its perfect acoustics.

The auditorium had filled up quickly, leaving Grace and the girls to take seats near the back—bad luck for the very nearsighted Zhanna. The quartet—Gordon, second violinist Urico Rossi, cellist Fritz Magg, and David—were performing the Boccherini Quartet in A Major, op. 33 no.6 the Bartok Quartet No. 6, and the Beethoven Quartet in F Major op.135. The players entered to applause and bowed. As they adjusted their music stands and tuned their instruments, it occurred to Zhanna that she had never heard a string quartet play, an odd gap in her extensive musical experience, largely due to the upheavals of the war. When the playing began, she was puzzled by something she heard.

It sounded so magnificent, so rich. I thought there was a French horn playing. I was looking for a horn but my eyes were so bad. Then it hit me: it was David. I did not know that a viola could make such an unearthly sound.

The party afterward was at the Washington home of Dr. and Mrs. McIlhenny, good friends of Larry and Grace. The doctor was out of town so Mrs. McIlhenny was hosting solo. Grace and the girls arrived first, and Zhanna grew nervous waiting for the members of the quartet—not about performing, if they were asked, but meeting them across the language barrier, especially David, the New York sophisticate in patent leather shoes. A knock at the front door sent Zhanna and Frina scurrying into the kitchen out of sight. Only David and Fritz Magg, the Viennese cellist he had met in the Army, were at the door. The quartet's violinists, Gordon and Rossi, had stayed behind. Mrs. McIlhenny coaxed the girls to make an entrance, but they were frozen in their shyness.

We would not step into the little dining room where Fritz and David were waiting for us. You could not move us. Mrs. McIlhenny finally pushed us through the swinging door and I just stood like a telephone pole with wide-open eyes, without any smile. Both of us just stood there like wild children. They were on the verge of bursting into laughter. It was the first time I saw David's face and I was amazed, absolutely amazed. I had never seen eyes so blue in my life.

After a few moments of awkward laughter and gesturing back and forth, Zhanna and Frina sat down at an upright piano in the cramped dining room. David and Fritz had introduced them to something new at the Coolidge Auditorium—string quartets— and now the girls would return the favor by performing their four-hand arrangement of Beethoven's *Egmont* Overture for orchestra, a staple of their wartime repertory. They positioned the sheet music and began to play.

David and Fritz stood up the whole time pointing
to the music and speaking fast. You could see on their
faces there was no end to their amazement and delight
to discover a four-hand arrangement of this great
composition which they knew thoroughly, but only
in the original. We didn't understand their exchange
but could tell they were satisfied with our spirited
performance. They laughed and we did too—the
enjoyment was contagious. We were finally back in our
kind of company.

They left early the next day under a pale blue sky for the trip back to Crozet. Zhanna was filled with a sense of exhilaration after replenishing her musical soul in the company of great artists. But she also was pierced by melancholy and loss; she had not wanted to leave. Zhanna gazed out the car window but did not see the passing countryside. She was hearing the unearthly tone of David's viola, and in her mind's eye she saw his eyes, the color of the sky.

Chapter Twenty-Seven

O ne day in early November, the memory of their brief furlough from the farm to visit Washington still fresh and beckoning as a dream interrupted, the girls heard a commotion outside and rushed to the front door. They could not believe their eyes.

Larry! At last!

It had been only six months since he had said good-bye at the Funk Kaserne displaced persons camp near Munich and assigned a member of his staff to drive the girls to Bremen in northern Germany to board the S.S. *Marine Flasher* for the journey to America. But it felt much longer. Just as one dog year is equal to seven human years, for Zhanna and Frina each month on the farm had seemed like a year as they waited for Larry to return home and resume his fostering of their musical destiny. None of them were cut out for farming, though only the girls had fully embraced that fact.

There were three steps on the long, white metal porch of the farmhouse. Larry came out of his vehicle, walked across the front lawn and put his foot on the first step.

Frina and I were on the third step waiting, and by the time Larry reached us the tears were streaming from our eyes with such speed that we couldn't speak.

Most soldiers returned from Europe with a satisfying sense of great mission accomplished. Larry arrived home with a burning urgency to resume a mission he had been forced to put on hold until he completed his military duties. He had not been home two weeks before sending a letter to the Peabody Conservatory of Music in Baltimore requesting an audition for Zhanna and Frina—a gambit of breathtaking audacity. Peabody was the oldest music conservatory in America, established in 1857, and among the most prestigious and selective alongside Juilliard, the Curtis Institute, and the Eastman School of Music. The notion that two teenage immigrants, in the country less than a year, with no training by recognized American teachers, would be granted an audition at Peabody—much less admitted—could only belong to an impossible dreamer.

Luckily, the girls had one on their side. Zhanna had seen Larry's dreams at work—getting her and Frina on the *Marine Flasher* when the U.S. had a zero quota for Russian immigrants was a small miracle. So she was not surprised when Larry told them to prepare for a trip to Baltimore to audition for a very famous man, though the name Reginald Stewart meant nothing to them. A Scotsman of regal bearing, Stewart was conductor of the Baltimore Symphony Orchestra and director of the Peabody, as well as a celebrated concert pianist. Larry cut the girls' farm chores and upped their time at the piano in the days leading up to the audition.

*Larry was in an excited state of mind because we
would be performing before a top-notch musician with
broad knowledge and education who would let us know
where we stood in the musical world—not exactly like
playing for ost workers in wartime Germany.*

Zhanna did not share Larry's agitation. She had never been nervous playing for musicians, even as a young girl auditioning for the hoary eminences of Soviet piano pedagogy. She felt a kinship and mutual respect with fellow musicians. It was the casual listener who didn't know a sharp from a flat that worried her. There was another reason Zhanna was serene on the eve of the audition. After living with the fear of betrayal for five years, she found that very little bothered her now. During the war she had welcomed Allied bombing of Berlin, where she was housed, and the strafing of trains taking her and other musicians to entertain *ost* workers at slave-labor camps around Germany.

*The bombs were a relief, a distraction from the greater
fear of being discovered as a Jew. If you die in bombing,
you are not humiliated. With betrayal, the persecution
is personal, a special torture like being thrown into a
grave with people who are still alive. Under the bombs,
we were all equal, Jews and non-Jews.*

Larry decided to leave the DeSoto in Crozet for Grace and take the train to Baltimore. For Zhanna, trains were still a symbol of danger and heartbreak, of forced evacuations and loss— from the train which carried away her dear friend, Irina, at the start of the war to the terrifying exodus out of Berlin in the final days of the war when she and Frina feared for their lives at the hands of bitter and humiliated German mob packed into the car with them. It was a measure of her preternatural resilience that Zhanna was nevertheless excited by the prospect of the trip to Baltimore. This was their first train ride in America in daylight. The trip from Grand Central Station to Crozet was at night, and they had been so exhausted from their arrival in New York that they fell asleep the moment they sat down and closed their eyes.

It was a mild autumn day and we were able to enjoy the scenery this time. Larry had spent countless hours in Germany telling us about the extraordinary qualities and uniqueness of America, and this was his chance to show us. He spent the whole time talking in his funny leftover German and pointing out the window, and we were comparing the great open expanses of Virginia to the landscape of Germany with small farms and extreme care in dividing the land. We had missed Larry's daily company so much.

The Peabody Conservatory occupies a Renaissance Revival building in the Mount Vernon neighborhood of Baltimore, situated among other magnificent specimens built by the rich and famous in the early decades of the nineteenth century when Baltimore was the fastest growing city in America.

We arrived before noon and found the center of town, or so it appeared to us, a well-kept square, very pretty;

*then we saw the Conservatory with a beautiful front
and rounded, decorative steps. There was a spacious
hallway inside leading to the audition room with a high
ceiling, tall windows, and two pianos.*

A shiver of déjà vu ran up Zhanna's spine.

*I was struck by how similar it was to Kharkov
Conservatory. I almost expected to see Professor Luntz
standing in the door of his studio, a roomy place with
two Bechsteins. It had large windows, and beautiful
natural light filtered through the foliage of the trees. He
was very tall with a wonderful large head, and every
time he illustrated a point was wondrous to us.*

It was the first time since coming to America that Zhanna
had thought of her beloved professor. He and his wife, Bella,
childless, had treated her and Frina as their own. It was the
Luntzes who gave their mother, Sara, a swath of blue silk to
make concert dresses for the girls when the Arshanskys had
no money. Professor Luntz always felt terrible guilt for not
saving the girls from the Germans. He should have taken
them when he and his wife fled east with so many other Jews!
But his guilt was misplaced. Not even Dmitri's brother-in-law,
Semyon, could persuade the Arshanskys to leave. Years later
when word filtered back to Kharkov that the girls had been
seen alive in Germany playing for *ost* workers, the professor
wept tears of joy.

After a few moments, an elegantly dressed man entered the

room alone and introduced himself as the director without giving his name. He was to be their jury of one.

He did not question Larry staying in the room. Then he asked us to play, one after another. He didn't ask for a lot of playing. He heard Bach, Beethoven, Chopin. He didn't specify his impressions. He just said he was satisfied and announced that we were accepted and would receive full scholarships. We were allowed to start right away. We were dying to go to the conservatory, to get into our old routine. We belonged to the conservatory!

The jubilant girls raced out of the audition room and down the stairs toward the street, laughing and chattering about their great fortune. They were going to study with great professors and be surrounded by students like themselves devoted to their art, just like in Kharkov. And best of all, their farming days were over!

Larry caught up with them and put his arms around their shoulders and grinned.

"It's *great* how well it went," he said. "What would you like to do next?"

"Lunch!" they cried.

Larry laughed and said, "This was a very good day, but now we are going to Juilliard."

Zhanna felt the blood drain from her face.

"What?! We cannot do it!" the sisters gasped.

"It's just interesting to see what they will think," Larry said.

But that was a playful lie. Juilliard was always his first choice, the Holy Grail—David's sacred training ground.

"Are we going *now*?" said Zhanna, her stomach growling for lunch.

"No, we have to have an appointment for an audition," Larry said.

He stood firmly and wouldn't listen to our protests. So we had to discard our fresh images of a school in America with a similar atmosphere to our beloved Kharkov Conservatory. Larry had no memories of Kharkov. We followed his decision because he had proven himself to us so unquestionably that our trust in him stopped us from fighting him. We knew the decision was made. We had to keep moving.

The girls were subdued on the train ride back to Crozet, deflated by Larry's bursting of their Peabody balloon. There was less conversation and more staring out the window at the countryside, growing browner and more denuded by the day. Zhanna was still dumbfounded by the events in Baltimore. She hoped Larry knew what he was doing. Their musical future was in the hands of a man who could barely read sheet music. How could he be sure they would even get an audition at Juilliard?

The way he dismissed the attention and approval of Reginald Stewart, this noted conductor and director of the Peabody, made me worry that we could be left on our own without any opportunity.

A few days after returning to Crozet, Larry gave the girls some news that lifted them out of their post-Peabody funk. "Uncle David," as he told them to call his viola-playing brother, was coming to spend Thanksgiving at the farm. The Gordon Quartet was taking a break from its busy tour schedule.

Zhanna had not forgotten the traumatic arrival in New York as a result of David's commitment to the Gordon String Quartet, but her memory of meeting David after the concert at the Library of Congress in Washington was much stronger. His broad, easy smile, his delight in her and Frina's four-hand arrangement of the Egmont Overture, and above all those blue eyes. . . .

We were very much excited with Uncle David's visit. Larry said he wanted to get to know us better. In Washington we had understood each other only when we played the Egmont Overture. *We asked if Uncle David was bringing his viola to the farm, but Larry didn't know.*

The after-concert party in Washington had been little more than a pleasant musical interlude and exchange of smiles—an overture to a simple friendship. David was at the farm for three days, but it took only one afternoon and evening for Zhanna to realize that he was anything but "formal," despite the patent leather shoes.

David turned out to have an irrepressible sense of
humor about everything. He made constant jokes, he
played with the Jarmans' two foster boys and was so
much fun just helping around the kitchen. After dinner,
Larry would do the dishes and give David a towel
to wipe them and the comedy hour would start with
David snapping the towel at us between each dish.
We laughed ourselves silly. Time went so quickly with
David around.

Except when it stood still for sports on the radio. Grace long ago had resigned herself to the sight of Larry and David huddled by the radio for hours listening to the squawky, scratchy broadcast of a ballgame, arguing and laughing, talking back to the voice on the radio. They worshipped at the temple of baseball—David was a Giants fan, Larry rooted for the hapless Senators—but any lesser god like football would do in the off-season. One day during the visit, Zhanna and Frina walked into a room and found the brothers glued to the broadcast of a Washington Redskins game. They would have been less baffled if they had come upon little green men from Mars doing "Macbeth" in Gaelic.

It was not possible to penetrate what was happening
no matter how we tried. We saw Larry and David
listening to a lot of hysterical screaming that was
coming out of the radio. They were totally absorbed,
often breaking into laughter then getting very upset. It
lasted so long. They were having a party of two. Grace

paid no attention to their doings. We would look in,
go out, and try to figure out what it all meant. This
was our first experience into the existence of sports
broadcasts—unknown in Russia. We thought it was
madness.

All was forgiven, though, because David had indeed brought his viola, as well as sheet music. Behind the towel-snapping jokester was an artist eager to gauge Zhanna's virtuosity. He chose a piece she had never played—Brahms' F-minor sonata for clarinet or viola. He put the music on the stand and picked up his viola.

He wanted me to play with him and it wasn't
important if I could not grasp it right away, to just
play. So we started, me entering an unknown jungle
and him knowing it cold. I hardly understood the
phrasing but kept going anyway so as not to get behind.
I played what I could grab, even if not in all my glory.
At the end he showed me a few things about the piece—
pointing to the music with his bow and illustrating
on his viola to hold a note longer or shorter. In music,
rhythm and counting are even more important than
sound. I knew almost no English, but I understood
"faster" and "slower."

He smiled and suggested that we try it again. I secretly
thought, "It's no use," but it made a little more sense
the second time. When the session ended I liked that he

wasn't patronizing to me. He understood that I couldn't
be proud of it so it would be useless to compliment
someone who has ears. I don't know how David
did it, but I wasn't totally discouraged. He showed
extraordinary patience and sophistication in not scaring
me off and managed to keep me encouraged enough so
the music would not stop. We played again the next day.

It would not be the last time. After three days on the farm, David packed up his viola, music, and silly jokes and headed back to New York for rehearsals with the Gordon Quartet, which was leaving soon on another concert tour.

The visit was the nicest time and it ended too soon.
From that time on, we had in mind one goal—to be
prepared for the decisive day. We had a date in January
to audition at Juilliard! Somehow, Larry had done it
again.

Chapter Twenty-Eight

Not once during David's visit at Thanksgiving did Grace ask him to help out around the farm. She knew it would be counterproductive. David had even less mechanical aptitude than Larry, if that was possible, and no interest in things agricultural. On his tour of the farm, it was clear he couldn't wait to get back to the house to break out his viola and sheet music. The question about David was not how to keep him down on the farm, but why bother?

When he left Charlottesville for New York at fourteen to study at Juilliard, it was almost as if David had been returning to his true native land after being mysteriously spirited away at birth to an alien hinterland. The teenage prodigy from small-town Virginia got to New York and never looked back. He delighted in the street life, worshipped the Giants, and melded seamlessly into the Jewish-dominated string culture at Juilliard. His admiring classmates told him he played like a Jew and took him home to their Jewish mothers for chicken soup and latkes.

David was in the first class admitted to the Juilliard School of Music, the 1926 marriage of two richly endowed institutions: the Institute for Musical Art, backed by banker James Loeb, and the Juilliard Graduate School, the legacy of textile merchant Augustus Juilliard. Among the celebrated faculty at the "new" Juilliard was cellist Felix Salmond, who with pianist Harold Bauer had heard David play at age twelve in Charlottesville and prophesied a brilliant future for the lad, though he probably was surprised to see David in the halls of Juilliard so soon.

By 1946, after being immersed in the city's musical life for nearly two decades, David was a New Yorker in all but accent, though his was more flat than Southern, except when it thickened for Southern jokes. When David learned that Zhanna and Frina were to audition at Juilliard, on his "home" turf, he appointed himself as a welcoming and search committee of one. His main concern, assuming the girls were admitted with scholarships—by no means a certainty—was that they have the right teacher. David was searching for two teachers: one at Juilliard and one who taught privately, just in case Juilliard said no.

The teacher he chose on the Juilliard faculty was Muriel Kerr, a celebrated pianist who had been a classmate of David's at the school. Kerr made her Carnegie Hall debut in 1928, performing Rachmaninoff's Concerto No. 2 with the New York Philharmonic, and then toured extensively in the U.S., Canada, and Europe. David became friends with Kerr's husband, cellist Naoum Benditzky, when they played together in the Coolidge Quartet before the war.

To David, Muriel's playing was magical. Her tone quality and control were extraordinary, and she was utterly free of ostentation. Like Rachmaninoff, Muriel was motionless at the piano—all her energy was poured into the music. Rachmaninoff once heard Muriel perform his second concerto and when asked his opinion, he said, "Don't change anything."

If the girls studied privately, David decided it would be with Walter Bricht, a Viennese immigrant and eclectic musical genius with equal abilities as a composer, pianist and vocal coach. David affectionately called him "Mickey Mouse" because his large ears stuck straight out from his bald head like antenna catching every stray note and melody in the air. But as much as David admired Bricht, it was unlikely the sisters would ever study with him. The Hebrew Immigrant Aid Society was prepared to cover their room and board, but only if they were studying at a conservatory as scholarship students. Unless he sold the farm, Larry could not afford to support the girls in New York. If Juilliard turned thumbs down, the girls would take the scholarship offer from Peabody, where Reginald Stewart would not have been amused to know he was being held in reserve as a backup to Juilliard.

The trips to Washington and Peabody and the music-making on the farm with David had fully awakened the sisters' artistic fire and ambition, which had gone into self-protective hibernation during the war when they feared each performance might be their last.

Now that our concerns of persecution were over, we could think of attending classes again, having regular lessons, and being able to meet other students and hear them play, even sit in on their lessons. What a joy! And the thought of going to the concert of an admired artist—that was peace time life. We could not wait

to start catching up after five years when learning
was lost to the unpredictable, the dangerous, and the
unspeakably brutal.

As Christmas neared, so did Larry's agitation and nervous excitement about the January audition. He busied himself with farm work and fought the urge to hover and kibitz as the girls practiced on the Steinway. It didn't matter that they had been offered full scholarships on the spot by the director of the Peabody Conservatory. In Larry's heart—seemingly disconnected from his ear—they were still the raw talents he discovered at Funk Kaserne in need of his expert instruction. Only eight months earlier, he had given a cautious assessment of their abilities in a letter to David, who could not have guessed that Larry was describing young pianists who had been accepted to Moscow State Conservatory with scholarships and had been playing publicly for years.

"I want to place their musical education in your hands until I get back," Larry wrote from Germany. "They stopped their studies at fourteen and twelve, and for four years played either none at all, or cheap theater stuff. They have now been practicing again only four months. But I believe they can be fine pianists."

It was an ironic situation. The Dawson who should have been coaching the sisters at this critical moment was David, not Larry. Larry had David's love for music, the same visceral connection, without any of his brother's artistry or knowledge. In Germany, out of respect and affection for their gung-ho savior, the girls humored Larry and tried to adopt some of his ideas without undoing techniques and principles learned from their master teachers at Kharkov Conservatory in Ukraine. Zhanna feared the result was sometimes odd.

> *After rehearsing for weeks we felt we were as ready*
> *as we would ever be for Juilliard. We were playing*
> *the same pieces as we did at Peabody—Bach and*
> *Beethoven—and a large part of them were learned*
> *with Larry giving his requests and instructions. I*
> *thought the jury would be plenty amazed by some of*
> *our exotic expressions of Beethoven sonatas. I cannot*
> *imagine what we sounded like.*

The audition was the second week of January 1947, five years to the month that Zhanna and Frina escaped the death march to Drobitsky Yar and began a journey of survival that seemed to have stretched over two lifetimes. The first lifetime was dead to them now, buried along with their parents, grandparents, and neighbors.

> *We never had any hope that they were still alive. After*
> *what we saw and experienced at the tractor factory*
> *where the Nazis kept us without food and water for*
> *two weeks before the march, we said goodbye to the idea*
> *that anyone was still alive.*

In New York they would be playing for coveted scholarships to Juilliard. That was the stated purpose of the audition. The immediate stakes were high. But their playing was now infused with a higher unstated purpose, with stakes beyond measure, a purpose inscribed in their souls—summoned from a place where children should never have to go.

Our music every time had saved us, snatched us out of the worst human pollution. That's what made our lives possible. Without it, we would have been destroyed long ago.

Arrangements were made for Lad and George to stay with the Jarmans so that Grace, who had missed the trip to Baltimore, could accompany Larry and the girls. It would be their first time in New York since the day they arrived. Their memory of the city was a blur. After waiting for hours at the pier for the tardy greeter dispatched by David, they had had only a few hours to window-shop on Fifth Avenue and buy a Russian-English dictionary before boarding the train for Crozet. Now, as the train wended its way north, Zhanna leafed through her dog-eared dictionary and realized it was time for a new copy. She thought of the Russian-speaking clerk at the bookstore who told the girls they had made a terrible mistake coming to America. How satisfying it would be to return to the bookstore with Juilliard scholarships in hand to answer the rude clerk—just as she rebuked the mocking Russian ballerinas in Kremenchug with her virtuosity on stage.

They would be in New York for two days, with the audition scheduled for the second day, after lunch. The train arrived at Grand Central around noon—everyone was starved. Larry took them to a sort of restaurant the girls had never seen before. Instead of sitting at a table, ordering, and having food delivered, they were expected to retrieve it themselves. They joined a long line of people with trays shuffling past what to Zhanna appeared to be a museum of food, a display of dishes stretching from one end of the room to the other. This wonderland of cuisine was called a cafeteria.

> *Frina and I were puzzled how people knew what to choose because there was no end to the choice. Sausages, potatoes, bread, pies of all kinds. It was a dilemma, and sure enough our eyes betrayed us and we couldn't begin to finish what we planned to eat. I was embarrassed before Larry and Grace to have such an overload of untouched food. There was nothing to do but try to swallow our misjudgments!*

The cafeteria feast was not the only new experience for Zhanna and Frina in New York. They had never stayed in a hotel or talked on a telephone. Grace did not have a phone in the farmhouse, and neither did her parents. Zhanna was dying to try out the phone in her hotel room—she sat on the bed running her finger around the rotary dial—but there was no one in America for her to call who spoke Russian. She got her chance when Larry called a friend in New York and after a few minutes, without warning, handed Zhanna the phone.

"Hello!" she shouted into the receiver, employing one of the few words in her arsenal of English, and a voice on the other end responded in kind. Zhanna beamed. Alexander Graham Bell was less thrilled when he made contact with Mr. Watson.

The next day, after a lighter lunch, they headed for Juilliard.

Under their winter coats, Zhanna and Frina wore plaid skirts, white blouses, and saddle oxfords—the outfit Grace had bought for their brief, ill-fated attendance at Greenwood High School. They had no idea what to expect at the school Larry had spoken of with such reverence and awe. A one-man jury as in Baltimore the month before? A panel of pedagogues like the one at Kharkov Conservatory that awarded the girls scholarships when they were eight and six years old? They had no idea what to expect.

The Juilliard building was situated near the corner of Broadway and 122nd Street. It was an old place, not primped up or outstanding in any way except that it had a lot of practice studios—many small ones with one upright piano, and teachers' studios with two pianos. The building itself couldn't compare to Peabody in appearance. But I was walking on clouds to return to the cacophony of practice rooms and young musicians polishing every sound in an endless variety of performances.

Larry and the girls (Grace decided to stay at the hotel) were ushered past a receptionist's desk up a flight of stairs to a hallway lined with studios. After a few tense minutes, a man emerged from the nearest studio and motioned for Zhanna and Frina to come inside. Larry was a nervous wreck, but Zhanna was strangely at ease, just as she had been six years before when auditioning for Professor Goldenweiser at Moscow State Conservatory when she was only thirteen. Zhanna was never nervous performing for other musicians; it was casual listeners with tin ears who terrified her. She was certain—but unconcerned—that the Juilliard professors would be amused by the bad habits and odd technique in her playing that came from five years of no instruction except Larry's antic kibitzing.

Larry was not allowed in the room as he had had at Peabody. We had a three-person jury—an elderly man and two women, a brunette and a blonde. Frina played first. One of the pieces was Beethoven's Sonata Opus 31 in D minor—"The Tempest". I played Bach's Partita in B-flat major and then Beethoven's "Appassionata". When I finished, the blonde woman got up quickly and came to the piano and moved me over a little bit to sit down. Before I could blink she was playing a few bars of the Partita in a way that seemed miraculously gorgeous and left me speechless. I didn't know why she did it or what she was trying to show me. I just knew that I wanted to play the way she did.

After the impromptu lesson, the girls were asked to wait outside in the hall with Larry, who was pacing up and down like an expectant father in a hospital. Zhanna's stomach should have been churning as the jury deliberated but, oddly, her mind was focused elsewhere. She could not stop thinking about the blonde juror's brilliant demonstration at the keyboard. Her reverie was broken by the voice of the gentleman juror, standing in the open doorway.

"We are ready to give you our decision," he said. "Mr. Dawson, please come in."

Larry entered the room a portrait of trepidation, his face a frown-smile mask of utter dread and high hope. He was in a much greater state of anxiety, ten times greater, than Zhanna and Frina out in the hall. The nattily dressed older juror addressed him.

"Mr. Dawson," he said, "I am Ernest Hutcheson, dean of the school. These are two members of our piano faculty, Rosalyn Tureck"—he nodded in the direction of the brunette—"and Muriel Kerr. We are pleased to offer the girls full scholarships to Juilliard."

Larry raised his arms and gave a triumphant little shout. The fondest dream of the impossible dreamer had come to fruition! He rushed over and shook hands with each juror. Then he turned and bolted out the door to the hallway where the girls were sitting on a bench idly chatting in Russian.

"*Yes!*" he exclaimed, startling them, "the jury said yes! You will by studying at Juilliard as full scholarship students! Can you believe it?"

Zhanna and Frina were almost as excited as Larry. They were standing in the hallway listening to Larry expound on the profound significance of the occasion when Hutcheson and the other jurors approached them.

"Excuse me," Hutcheson said, "but there is one more thing I need to tell the girls." He turned to them. "Miss Kerr will be your teacher."

Zhanna was stunned. She looked at Hutcheson as if she had not heard him correctly. This remarkable pianist was to be her teacher? Winning the scholarship suddenly became a secondary reward. Zhanna had won other scholarships. But she had never heard a pianist like Muriel.

This was the prize announcement to me—a fantastic teacher. When Muriel sat down next to me and played the Bach Partita, there were sparkles in my ears and eyes. I couldn't wait for our first lesson!

The train back to Crozet left in late afternoon as the meek January sun was surrendering to dusk. By the time they crossed into New Jersey, darkness had fallen. All Zhanna saw in the window was her reflection, staring inward. She was exhausted but her mind was a riot of images and thoughts and sensations from the day in New York when her life had changed forever. When would she see Muriel again? Is it possible David had arranged for her to be on the jury? How she wished Professor Luntz had been there! Who would tell Reginald Stewart they were spurning his generous offer? When would she see David again so she could tell him the wonderful news?

As Zhanna lay back and closed her eyes, she replayed the audition and her thoughts drifted to another performance—the concert in Germany after the war for 1,200 death-camp survivors. It seemed a hundred years ago, but it had been only nine months. The concert had been Larry's brainchild, naturally, and he had designed the impossibly long and difficult program for Zhanna and Frina.

We said "yes" instantly, knowing very well that we could not present a concert with polished results. Our

*lifetime training and quest for perfection was put on
the back burner. When we found ourselves auditioning
in the most prestigious music school in America, we
turned back to our need for quality and refinement. For
the survivors, how we played was less important than
the event. Their presence alone was a concert without
sounds.*

*Beethoven, Mendelssohn, Brahms, Liszt, and Schubert
were all there for us. They all came to celebrate our
freedom. That's the way these composers wanted
Germany and the world to be. Our mother, father,
grandfather, and grandmother were there, too. They
came alive to listen and celebrate with us.*

Zhanna was succumbing at last to exhaustion and the rocking of the train. The tapestry of images was slowing now, dis-
solving from her consciousness like breath on a windowpane. All
that remained was the shadow of an inextinguishable memory.

*Father is next to me on the road, he is placing his coat
over my shoulders, he is whispering to me.
"I don't care what you do—just live!"*

Epilogue

The fates of the two child prodigies, one from Ukraine, the other from Virginia, continued their remarkable parallel paths. Zhanna's first chamber music teacher at Juilliard was Felix Salmond, who forty years earlier had marveled at thirteen-year-old David's virtuosity in his public debut in Charlottesville. In the summer of 1947, their parallel paths narrowed and finally converged, nine months after their first meeting in Washington, D.C.

On a mountaintop in the Berkshires, not far from the Gordon Quartet's summer venue at Music Mountain, David proposed. And Zhanna disposed. How could she say no to those blue eyes, to that unearthly tone? She was not looking for a husband, she told David. She wanted to be a student and concentrate on her music. Besides, she had two other suitors by now: a Jewish banker's son—granted, she couldn't stand him—and a gentleman from an elite family who one day would be mayor of Charlottesville. Two days after Zhanna said no, David resumed dating an old girlfriend who had been his viola student. Zhanna was on his doorstep the next day. "I absolutely could not let that witch get her nails into him," she said. "That is when I discovered my great attachment to David."

David, thirty-four, and Zhanna, twenty, were married December 14, 1947, in Hackensack, N.J., with David's musical hero and former maestro of the Minneapolis Symphony, Dimitri Mitropoulos, among the guests. Zhanna's hero, Muriel Kerr, played Schubert's G-flat Major Impromptu at the reception in a New York apartment.

Soon after their wedding, David was playing in the NBC Symphony under Arturo Toscanini when he accepted a position at Indiana University as a teacher and a member of the Berkshire String Quartet in 1948. Zhanna later joined the IU faculty as a teacher while pursuing a solo career and performing with the Berkshire String Quartet in Bloomington and at Music Mountain, which became the quartet's summer home after the Gordon Quartet disbanded. David and Zhanna also performed together for many years, while raising two sons, my brother Bill and myself.

After Juilliard, Frina studied with legendary teacher Sidney Foster at Indiana University, where she met Kenwyn Boldt, also a student of Foster's. They were married in 1955 and for many years were among the most celebrated four-hand piano teams in America, in addition to performing solo. Both were on the faculty at the State University of New York, Buffalo, where Frina later served as chairman of the piano department. The Boldts are now retired and living in Wisconsin. They have two sons, David and Steven, and three grandchildren.

My father died in 1975 at age sixty-two of cigarette-induced emphysema and heart disease. Larry took a job in the State Department in immigration affairs in 1947, thus saving himself and his family from a life in farming. Every night he played the kids to sleep with the "Moonlight" Sonata. Larry died in 1987 at age seventyseven. Grace is in robust health at eighty-eight and lives on a horse farm named Windchase in Virginia with her youngest daughter, Phyllis, a member of 1988 U.S. Olympic Equestrian team. In 2006, Phyllis bought a chestnut gelding of "extravagant and ethereal movement," a horse that "floats over the ground." She named him "Fantasy Impromptu."

As my mother and Frina were making new lives for themselves in America, they were the subjects of an ongoing drama they knew nothing about. It was widely presumed that they had perished with the rest of their family at Drobitsky Yar. Unbeknownst to them, their names were listed among the dead at the Yad Vashem Holocaust Memorial in Israel. As recently as 1995, a Russian-born radio journalist in Israel was telling listeners the tale of the two sisters, piano prodigies, lost in the war. There were two people who refused to accept that ending to the story, who never gave up hope of finding the sisters alive: their cousin, Tamara, and Zhanna's Kharkov classmate, Irina, who still had three postcards Zhanna gave her in 1941 before Irina's family fled east to escape the invading Germans.

"So long from me forever," Zhanna wrote. *"Please never forget me."*

Irina never forgot, and never stopped searching for Zhanna and Frina, placing ads in Russian-language newspapers in New York and contacting international refugee organizations. Tamara was searching, too, from Israel where she had immigrated after the war. Living just hours apart in Israel, neither knew that the other was searching; both kept running into dead ends.

It took a chance meeting in 1978 in Buffalo, N.Y., to begin to unlock the mystery. Izaak and Tilia Zaslawsky had known Zhanna and Frina when they were all students together in Kharkov. In 1977, the Zaslawskys left Kharkov for Brooklyn where Izaak, a distinguished violinist, joined an orchestra of Russian immigrants. Frina and Ken were in the audience when the orchestra performed in Buffalo in 1978. Frina was intrigued when the conductor introduced the players, including a violinist from Kharkov. She approached Izaak backstage after the concert.

"Do you know me?" she asked him. "I am Frina Arshanskaya."

Izaak thought he had seen a ghost. They reminisced for hours that night, a conversation that spanned forty years of memories and tumultuous history. Slowly over the next 20 years, bit by bit, the news that my mother and Frina were alive reached friends and relatives abroad.

One day in 1995, the phone rang at my mother's home in Atlanta. It was her cousin Tamara calling from Israel. For fifty years, neither had known the other had survived. Assuming that her Americanized cousin no longer spoke Russian, Tamara addressed her in English. Suspicious, Zhanna hung up on her. Tamara kept calling. Not until the fourth call, when Tamara switched to Russian, did my mother believe it was really her cousin. Tamara sent my mother the family photos that appear in this book. It was the first time I had ever seen pictures of my grandparents and of my mother as a little girl.

After Tamara's call to my mother in 1995, it took another six years for the news to reach Irina, whose zeal for the search was undimmed despite decades of futility. "The postcard and a photo of the two sisters were always with me wherever I went," she said, "from Siberia to Kiev, then to Donezk, and finally to Israel. All those years, more than sixty years, I was mourning their fate." But clearly she could never accept it.

Then, one day in 2001, on a hunch she phoned Irina Babitch, an Israeli journalist from Kharkov, to ask if she knew anything about the Arshanskaya sisters. Yes, Babitch said, they are alive and living in the U.S. "From that moment it became an obsession of mine to find them," Irina said.

And soon she did. The girlhood friends who spent so many happy hours strolling arm-in-arm down the leafy boulevards in Kharkov had a joyous reunion on the phone. Irina sent my mother a copy of the postcards from a lifetime ago. Today they are among my mother's most treasured possessions. Irina, though, mourns the loss of the precious photo of Zhanna and Frina which did not survive the dislocations of life.

"We have moved from one city to another with all the un-avoidable shaking up of all our belongings," she wrote in "The Lost Photo," which appeared in an Israeli newspaper. "Many times I overturned the books on my bookshelves searching for it. Alas! But it is not the biggest loss in our lives. We are alive. We keep on living in spite of all."

In 2006, I traveled with my wife, Candy, to Ukraine to see my mother's homeland for the first time and do research for this book. My mother declined our invitation to accompany us—she has never gone back—but was enthusiastic about the journey and gave us a note of introduction, in Russian, explaining who we were and giving a brief history of the Arshanskys. We handed out copies to everyone we met—hotel clerks, flower vendors, cabbies, fellow travelers on trains and buses—and my mother's words invariably transformed suspicious stares into smiles and often tears. "Dear Countrymen!" it began, "I am turning to you because my son Greg and his wife Candy don't know the language—it is in case they need help," and ended, "Thank you all for generosity and colossal courage. Be happy and healthy. Zhanna Arshanskaya Dawson, who also would love to be going to see you all."

In many ways it was a joyous and fulfilling journey. We visited Berdyansk, the lovely seaside town where she was born, and Kharkov, where she spent much of her childhood and studied at the music conservatory. We were welcomed into the same home on Katsarskaya Street where my mother was given refuge by the family of her shy schoolmate, Nicolai Bogancha. In 2008, Nicolai's parents, Prokofy and Yevdokia, were formally recognized as Righteous Gentiles ("Righteous Among the Nations") by Yad Vashem for their act of heroism. Nicolai's widow, Antonina, still lives in that home and served us a Ukrainian feast on the same beautiful dishes my mother and Frina used more than sixty years ago. But not all the trip was celebratory.

We made the somber pilgrimage to Drobitsky Yar, outside Kharkov, where the Nazis murdered at least fifteen thousand Jews including Zhanna and Frina's parents and paternal grandparents. The prominence of death camps such as Auschwitz and Treblinka as symbols of the Holocaust has overshadowed the fact that the Final Solution as we know it—the systematic mass slaughter of Jews—began not in the Zyklon-B showers of Auschwitz but in open fields in Ukraine at places such as Babi Yar and Drobitsky Yar.

Likewise, because of the Nuremberg war trials from 1945 to 1949, which trained an international spotlight on the architects and executioners of the Holocaust, it is little known that the first trial of Nazis for crimes against humanity was conducted by the Soviets in Kharkov in 1943. Three German officers and a Ukrainian collaborator were convicted and hanged in the public square on December 19, 1943. Photos of the event are on display at the Kharkov Holocaust museum, the first such museum in Ukraine when it was founded in 1996 by a group of brave activists led by Larisa Volovik, without support from the government.

In 2002, the Drobitsky Yar Committee dedicated a memorial in the expanse of sloping fields where the Nazis disposed of bodies in shallow ravines. Today, the fields are overgrown, but history lurks just beneath the pastoral tableau. Recent digging unearthed German weapons and bleached bones. Our guide, Irina, said, "I see strawberries and cranberries growing in the ravines, and it reminds me of blood."

Part of the austerely beautiful memorial complex at Drobitsky Yar is a subterranean "Room of Tragedy" with the names of victims etched on the walls in long columns of Cyrillic. Thus far, only 4,300 names have been put on the wall, so I was somewhat surprised to find the names of my grandparents and great-grandparents. I was *shocked* to find the names of my mother and Frina, engraved with equal certainty and finality. They had come that close to extinction. I had come that close to non-existence.

It was like visiting a cemetery and coming upon my own grave-stone.

My mother, now eighty-one, was heroic in ransacking her memory and her boxes of papers and photos to make this book possible. But, inevitably, memories fade and documents vanish. In early 2007, as I was completing revisions of the manuscript, I received a call from a childhood friend who said she had come across a yellowed, typewritten document about my mother which she thought I would find interesting. Our families had been close, and apparently my parents had shared the document with hers.

Undated but likely produced in the mid-1950s, the self-described "affidavit" is titled "Janna Dawson's story as told to David Dawson," my father. It's a capsule version of her war story, ending in Germany after V-E Day. When I told my mother about it on the phone, she drew a blank. Only when she saw a copy did she remember its purpose. After the war, the German government established a fund to compensate Holocaust survivors, and required "plaintiffs" to submit affidavits enumerating their losses and suffering.

Zhanna and Frina lost both parents, two grandparents, and their country. They were awarded $800 each.

"It was the first money I ever had," my mother said. "I think the lawyer took as much as we did."

She said it without bitterness. As my mother has resurrected and relived these memories over the past several years, I have heard in her voice sorrow and pain and anger—anger sometimes curdling into quiet rage. But I have never heard bitterness or cynicism. Larry was right. She and Frina saw the filthiest and

worst things, and came through it pure as gold. But not un-
changed.

> *Somehow the story, the history, went around us instead*
> *of through us. It is a miraculous thing because anything*
> *could have been done to us at any moment in those five*
> *years. We did not remain the same, I assure you.*

Coda

On October 24, 1950, Vladimir Horowitz came to Bloomington to perform at the Indiana University Auditorium. For Zhanna, in the audience, it seemed that fate had come full circle. The Holocaust had consumed her old life in Russia and set her on a tortuous path, ten years and ten thousand miles long, leading to this serendipitous rendezvous with her countryman and hero.

The auditorium manager gave me a seat in the first
row. I was right under Horowitz's hands. He taught
me a lesson as he played because I was working on
the same Scarlatti sonata. It was so difficult. I had to
throw my left hand over the right one very fast, and
sometimes I didn't hit the right note. I saw that when
Horowitz crossed his left hand over his arm, he never
bent his fingers—never. So I did the same thing, and I
never made the mistake again.

Afterward, Zhanna stood in line backstage to thank Horowitz and to briefly reminisce about studying with his sister Regina in Kharkov. Others in line carried programs for Horowitz to sign. Not Zhanna.

I never ask artists to sign their names. I want to say something to them, learn from them. There was a long, long line for Horowitz. I watched him sitting at the desk. Everyone pushed their little programs at him and he kept writing and writing, never lifting his head. When my turn came, I just stood there. His eyes were still fixed on the spot of the desk where people placed their programs. When there was nothing to write on he lifted his head and looked at me, and I was dead. His eyes were so fantastic—black, shiny eyes. The light jumped out at me. I thought the sparkles were going to fall out on me. All I could get out of my mouth was, "Spasiba" (thank you). He stood up, looked at me, took my hand, and kissed it. I almost lost my steadiness.

Horowitz, who left Russia in 1925 to pursue his career, did not return until 1986 for his memorable homecoming concert in Moscow. My mother never returned, but she has revisited long-buried memories to tell the full story of her extraordinarily tragic and triumphant life.

On behalf of her four grandchildren—Chris, Aimee, David, Anna Sophia—and all grandchildren, may I say, to steal her simple eloquence—Spasiba.

Zhanna and Frina's Repertory During the War

ZHANNA'S SOLO REPERTORY

Beethoven
"Pathetique" Sonata
"Appassionata" Sonata

Chopin
Waltz Brilliant, Opus 34 in A-Flat Major
Waltz No. 14 in E Minor
Etude Op. 10, No. 5
Nocturne Op. 9, No.1
Etude in F Minor
Fantasy Impromptu, Opus 66 in C-Sharp Minor
Scherzo in B-Flat Minor

Liszt
Hungarian Rhapsody No. 11
La Chasse (from Transcendental Etudes) No. 12

Grieg
Concerto in A Minor, Op. 16

Mendelsohnn
Scherzo Capriccio

Rachmaninoff
Prelude in C Minor

FRINA'S SOLO REPERTORY

Beethoven
Sonata in D Minor, Op. 31 ("The Tempest")

Rachmaninoff
Prelude in G Minor

Beethoven
Egmont Overture

Schubert
Military Marches Op. 51
Peer Gynt Suite

Brahms
Hungarian Dances

Liszt
Hungarian Rhapsodie, No. 2

Bibliography

Ailsby, C., *Images of Barbarossa* (Brassey's Inc., 2001)

Dean, M., *Collaboration in the Holocaust* (St. Martin's Press, 2000)

Dobroszycki, L., and Gurock, J., *The Holocaust in the Soviet Union* (M.E. Sharpe, Inc., 1993)

Elliott, M., *Pawns of Yalta* (University of Illinois Press, 1982)

Gitelman, Z., *Bitter Legacy* (Indiana University Press, 1997)

Morris, M., *Stalin's Famine and Roosevelt's Recognition of Russia* (University Press of America, 1994)

Potichnyj, P., and Aster, H., *Ukrainian-Jewish Relations in Historical Perspective* (Canadian Institute of Ukrainian Studies, 1988)

Rubenstein, J., and Altman, I., *The Unknown Black Book* (Indiana University Press, 2008)

Tolstoy, N., *Stalin's Secret War* (Holt, Rinehart and
  Winston, 1982)
Wyman, M., *Europe's Displaced Persons, 1945-1951*
  (Cornell University Press, 1998)
Ziemke, E., *The Red Army 1918-1941* (Taylor & Francis
  Books, 2004)
Zipperstein, S., *Imagining Russian Jewry* (University of
  Washington Press, 1999)

Acknowledgments

There were two main obstacles to the writing of this book: a reluctant subject and a doubtful author. My mother was reluctant to revisit and plumb memories she had never shared. I was doubtful that writing 15-inch newspaper columns for 40 years had equipped me to do book-length justice to a story of such horror, beauty and consequence.

Because maternal love trumps reluctance, the first obstacle was easily surmounted. I asked—my mother said yes. My own doubt proved more stubborn. It took a small village of loving family, supportive friends, kind strangers, and patient professionals to push me, and this project across the finish line of an eight-year marathon. Whether I did justice to the story is left to the jury of my readers.

What follows is a necessarily abbreviated list of the many people who helped, in big and small ways, to bring this project to fruition. To all of them I owe gratitude and more:

My friend and colleague, Jean Patteson, an elegant writer and discerning reader, for administering an early cold shower and informing me that what I thought was a finished manuscript was really "a good outline" for a book.

Darryl Owens, another gifted colleague, for hooking me up with Tina Jacobson, my indefatigable agent.

Pegasus Books publisher Claiborne Hancock for the courage and audacity to hope there was room for one more Holocaust memoir.

Jessica Case, my brilliant editor, who is too young to know how rare she is.

Mark Pinsky, friend and author, for helping me navigate the unfathomable waters of the publishing world.

Cindy Worth and Patti Campbell, who gamely waded through a maze of Russian names and places to produce interview transcripts.

Grace and Phyllis Dawson for the stories and photos of my uncle Larry Dawson, which only they could provide.

My mother's cousin Tamara in Israel, for her memories and the priceless Arshansky family photos I had no idea existed. Ada, another cherished friend from my mother's childhood.

Larissa Volovik, brave founder of the Holocaust museum in Kharkov, her daughter Yulana and granddaughter Sofiya.

The Bogancha family in Kharkov: Antonina, her daughter, Larissa , son-in-law Vadim, and granddaughter Mariana.

Poet Theodore Deppe, my friend since grade school, for his haunting and beautiful poem "Music School" which graces the first pages of the book.

My son, Chris, and daughter, Aimee, for their constant love and unconditional enthusiasm.

Tess Wise, Eva Ritt, Harriett and Hy Lake, Alan and Kelly

Ginsburg, Bob and Judy Yarmuth, and other members of the Orlando Jewish community whose passionate commitment to preserving the memories and lessons of the Holocaust sustained and inspired me.

The book would be a pale version of itself without the presence, seen and unseen, of Irina Vlodavsky, my mother's great friend with whom she was reunited after 60 years, just in time to make her indispensable contribution. In addition to material from her published story, "The Lost Photo," Irina provided historical context and insights, and a keen editor's eye to the manuscript.

I first became aware of the full dimensions of my mother's remarkable story in 1978 when I interviewed her for a newspaper article to coincide with airing of the NBC miniseries "Holocaust." The material cried out for book treatment, but over the ensuing 20 years the reluctant subject and doubtful author pretended not to hear the call, hoping the idea would fade away.

You are holding this book today because of two people who refused to let that happen. One is the great journalist and inimitable writer Bob Hammel—my friend, my mentor, my standard - the high bar I ever strive for but never reach. Once every couple of years, Bob would pointedly remind me, "You've got to do that book."

More frequent prodding came from Candy - my wife, best friend, web mistress, and partner every step of the way. She was my biggest critic and cheerleader, offering penetrating critiques and new angles of the story to explore. She persuaded me that we needed to visit Ukraine to gain a feel for my mother's words, and helped me overcome my journalistic remove to find the emotional heart of the story.

Finally, and most important, the reluctant subject herself, without whom none of us would have had the privilege to work on a project which adds a unique chapter to the history of the Holocaust. In her retrieving and articulating of terrible memories, her tireless rehearsal of events, and meticulous annotation of manuscripts, I witnessed the character and determination that made her a piano virtuoso—and survivor.

Thanks, Mom—it's been an honor getting to know you all over again.